# Norfolk: A Birdwatcher's Site Guide

Phil Benstead, Steve Rowland and Richard Thomas

Shoebill

Published by Shoebill Books, 59 Coolidge Gardens, Cottenham, Cambridge CB4 8RQ

# Norfolk: A Birdwatcher's Site Guide

by Phil Benstead, Steve Rowland and Richard Thomas

Copyright © Shoebill Books 2001

ISBN 0 9528065 1 7

Shoebill

Cover photograph by Steve Rowland

Printed by Crowes, Norwich, Norfolk

# Acknowledgements

Many people have  helped with the creation of *Norfolk: A Birdwatcher's Site Guide*, far too many to mention here individually.

However, we would like to thank the many wardens and site managers who read through and commented on drafts of site accounts to "their" reserves.

We would also like to make a special mention of Neil Bowman for the use of his wonderful back cover picture of a Bittern, Jane Kohler for her help with sorting out legal matters in setting up Shoebill, and a special thank you to Kathleen Rosewarne for carefully proof-reading and commenting on two sets of proofs.

Any mistakes or inaccuracies in the text are, of course, the sole responsibility of the authors.

# Contact us

We hope that *Norfolk: A Birdwatcher's Site Guide* will help you to get the most out of your birdwatching in this special county.

All of the sites in this book have been visited by the authors and the site managers consulted, but over time some details will inevitably change.

We would like to hear from you with any updates to the information presented here, and to receive information on sites not featured that might be suitable for inclusion in any future editions.

Please send your comments to:

Richard Thomas,
59 Coolidge Gardens,
Cottenham,
Cambridge CB4 8RQ.

Email shoebill.books@ntlworld.com

Thank you, and have a great time birdwatching in Norfolk...

# Contents

Chapter 1: West Norfolk ........................................................ 5

    1.01 Hunstanton .............................................................. 6
    1.02 Heacham ................................................................. 7
    1.03 Snettisham ............................................................. 8
    1.04 Dersingham Bog (a) and Wolferton (b) ............................ 10
    1.05 Flitcham and Abbey Farm ....................................... 11
    1.06 Fishers Fleet (a) and Lynn Point (b) ........................... 12
    1.07 Roydon Common .................................................. 13
    1.08 Massingham Heath ................................................ 15
    1.09 Pentney Gravel Pits .............................................. 16
    1.10 Tottenhill Gravel Pits ........................................... 17
    1.11 Welney .................................................................. 18
    1.12 Ouse Washes ........................................................ 19

Chapter 2: North Norfolk ................................................... 21

    2.01 Holme NOA (a) and NWT (b) reserves ...................... 23
    2.02 Titchwell Marsh .................................................. 26
    2.03 Choseley Area ..................................................... 28
    2.04 Burnham Norton .................................................. 29
    2.05 Holkham .............................................................. 30
    2.06 Holkham Hall ...................................................... 32
    2.07 Wells Woods ........................................................ 33
    2.08 Warham Greens ................................................... 34
    2.09 Stiffkey Woods .................................................... 35
    2.10 Stiffkey Fen ........................................................ 36
    2.11 Blakeney Point and Harbour ................................. 37
    2.12 Cley Marshes ...................................................... 38
    2.13 Walsey Hills ........................................................ 40
    2.14 Salthouse Beach Road .......................................... 41
    2.15 Salthouse Heath .................................................. 42
    2.16 Kellings Quags .................................................... 43
    2.17 Swanton Novers ................................................... 44

Chapter 3: East Norfolk and the Broads ................................................. 45

3.01 Gunton Lakes ................................................................. 47
3.02 Barton Broad ................................................................. 48
3.03 Blickling Lake ................................................................ 49
3.04 Sparham Pools .............................................................. 50
3.05 Waxham ....................................................................... 52
3.06 Hickling Broad .............................................................. 53
3.07 Horsey Mere ................................................................. 55
3.08 Martham Broad .............................................................. 57
3.09 Winterton Dunes ........................................................... 58
3.10 How Hill Nature Reserve ................................................ 59
3.11 Ranworth Broad ............................................................ 60
3.12 Flegg Broads (Ormesby, Rollesby and Filby Broads) ......... 62
3.13 Surlingham Church Marsh .............................................. 63
3.14 Rockland Broad ............................................................ 64
3.15 Strumpshaw Fen ........................................................... 66
3.16 Buckenham and Cantley Marshes ................................... 68
3.17 Cantley Sugar Factory ................................................... 70
3.18 Berney Marshes ............................................................ 71
3.19 Breydon Water .............................................................. 73
3.20 Great Yarmouth ............................................................ 74
3.21 Chedgrave and Langley Marshes ................................... 76
3.22 Hardley Flood .............................................................. 77

Chapter 4: The Brecks ................................................................. 79

4.01 Wayland Wood ............................................................. 80
4.02 Thompson Water ........................................................... 81
4.03 Lynford Arboretum ....................................................... 82
4.04 Lakenheath ................................................................. 83
4.05 Weeting Heath ............................................................. 84
4.06 Santon Downham ......................................................... 86
4.07 East Wretham .............................................................. 87
4.08 Mayday Farm ............................................................... 88
4.09 Thetford Warren ........................................................... 89
4.10 Barnhamcross Common ................................................ 91

Norfolk species list ................................................................... 93
Useful addresses ...................................................................... 98
Classifieds .............................................................................. 103

# Introduction

Welcome to *Norfolk: A Birdwatcher's Site Guide*, the first comprehensive guide to Norfolk, arguably the UK's foremost birdwatching county. All of the authors are birdwatchers with extensive Norfolk experience and we are pleased to be able to share our knowledge and enthusiasm with you.

We have tried to make this guide as comprehensive as possible by including the star sites, such as Titchwell and Cley Marshes, alongside lesser known but still very interesting places. We have exercised caution about the places included in the guide – some sites are in sensitive areas that would suffer from undue disturbance. We have also sought expert advice before including breeding sites for rare species and there are a few places that have been excluded at the request of the relevant site managers.

Many of the locations covered are nature reserves. If you want further information about any of these, we strongly encourage you to contact the relevant organisation. To help you with this, we have included an almanac of useful contacts and addresses for organisations concerned with birds, nature conservation and tourism in Norfolk. We also have invited some local businesses to advertise in the book. If you find this service helpful, please mention Shoebill when replying to adverts.

Birdwatchers who visit Norfolk have a high public profile and are important ambassadors for conservation. They are very welcome in Norfolk, and the money they spend is vital to the local economy. However, please observe the Country Code and the Birdwatchers' Code of Conduct, which are reproduced below, and respect the rights of local people. We strongly recommend that you buy a set of Ordnance Survey maps to Norfolk. The map references in the text are taken from these. The relevant maps in the Landranger series are: 132, 133, 134, 143, 144 and 156.

Finally, if you have enjoyed your birdwatching in Norfolk, please consider supporting one or more of the conservation organisations which are active in the county, and don't forget to submit your bird records to the County Recorder.

## The Country Code
Enjoy the countryside and respect its life and work
Guard against all risk of fire. Fasten all gates
Keep your dog under close control
Keep to public paths across farmland
Use gates and stiles to cross fences, hedges and walls
Leave livestock, crops and machinery alone
Take your litter home. Help to keep all water clean
Protect wildlife, plants and trees
Take special care on country roads. Make no unnecessary noise

*(Reprinted with permission from the Countryside Agency)*

# The Birdwatcher's Code of Conduct

## 1 Welfare of birds must come first
Whether your particular interest is photography, ringing, sound recording, scientific study or just birdwatching, remember that the welfare of birds must always come first.

## 2 Habitat protection
A bird's habitat is vital to its survival, and therefore we must ensure that our activities do not cause damage.

## 3 Keep disturbance to a minimum
Birds' tolerance of disturbance varies between species and seasons. Therefore, it is safer to keep all disturbance to a minimum. No birds should be disturbed from the nest in case the opportunities for predators to take eggs or young are increased. In very cold weather, disturbance to birds may cause them to use vital energy at a time when food is difficult to find. Wildfowlers impose bans during cold weather: birdwatchers should exercise similar discretion.

## 4 Rare breeding birds
If you discover a rare breeding bird and feel that protection is necessary, inform the appropriate RSPB Regional Officer, or the Species Protection Department at The RSPB, The Lodge, Sandy, Beds SG19 2DL. Otherwise, it is best in almost all circumstances to keep the record strictly secret to avoid disturbance by other birdwatchers and attacks by egg-collectors. Never visit known sites of rare breeding birds unless they are adequately protected. Even your presence may give away the site to others and cause so many other visitors that the birds may fail to breed successfully. Disturbance at or near the nest of species listed on the First Schedule of the Wildlife and Countryside Act 1981 is a criminal offence.

## 5 Rare migrants
Rare migrants or vagrants must not be harassed. If you discover one, consider the circumstances carefully before telling anyone. Will an influx of birdwatchers disturb the bird or others in the area? Will the habitat be damaged? Will problems be caused with the landowner?

## 6 The law
The bird protection laws, as now embodied in the Wildlife and Countryside Act 1981, are the result of hard campaigning by previous generations of birdwatchers. As birdwatchers, we must abide by them at all times and not allow them to fall into disrepute.

## 7 Respect the rights of landowners

The wishes of landowners and occupiers of land must be respected. Do not enter land without permission. Comply with permit schemes. If you are leading a group, do give advance notice of the visit, even if a formal permit scheme is not in operation. Always obey the Country Code.

## 8 Respect the rights of other people

Have proper consideration for other birdwatchers. Try not to disrupt their activities or scare birds they are watching. There are many people who also use the countryside. Do not interfere with their activities and, if it seems that what they are doing is causing unnecessary disturbance to birds, do try to take a balanced view. Flushing gulls when walking a dog on the beach may do little harm, while the same dog might be a serious disturbance at a tern colony. When pointing this out to a non-birdwatcher, be courteous but firm. A non-birdwatcher's goodwill towards birds must not be destroyed by the attitude of birdwatchers.

## 9 Keeping records

Much of today's knowledge about birds is the result of meticulous record keeping by our predecessors. Make sure you help to add to tomorrow's knowledge by sending records to your county bird recorder.

## 10 Birdwatching abroad

Behave abroad as you would at home. This code should be firmly adhered to when abroad (whatever the local laws). Well behaved birdwatchers can be important ambassadors for bird protection.

*(Reprinted with permission from the RSPB)*

# Chapter 1: West Norfolk

## Introduction

West Norfolk is comparatively underwatched compared to the better-known north Norfolk. However, the birdwatching in west Norfolk is truly outstanding, with the chance to see huge numbers of birds. Each winter the mudflats and saltmarshes of the Wash are home to more than 300,000 birds, making it the UK's most important avian estuary. There are few greater birdwatching spectacles than the sight of swirling clouds of tens of thousands of waders flying over the Wash on a winter's morning or the dawn flight of thousands of Pink-footed Geese leaving their roost site. Inland the agricultural landscape is dominated by sugar beet, the basis for winter foraging for the geese.

The Wash

N

0 — 4 miles

1.01
1.02
1.03
1.04a
1.04b
1.05
1.06b
1.07   1.08
1.06a
Kings Lynn
1.09
1.10
Wisbech
Downham Market
1.11
1.12

## Special birds

West Norfolk hosts several bird species that are scarce elsewhere in the county. These include Pink-footed Geese, seaduck, including scoter, Eiders and Long-tailed Ducks, and Purple Sandpipers. Breeding birds include Tree Sparrows, Grey Partridges, Fulmars, Nightingales and Nightjars. Fishers Fleet in King's Lynn offers some of the best gull watching in Norfolk and is a good place to look for Yellow-legged and Glaucous Gulls.

## Timing

Winter is the time to see flocks of Pink-footed Geese, spectacular high-tide flights of waders, and hunting Hen Harriers and Barn Owls on the Wash. This is also the time to look for Smew at Tottenhill Gravel Pits and gulls at King's Lynn. Off Hunstanton, scan the sea for flocks of seaducks and search the groynes at high tide for roosting Purple Sandpipers.

A visit in early spring will reward you with the first summer migrants, and a little later on Nightingales will be in full song on Roydon Common.

Summer is a great time to watch the nesting colonies of Black-headed Gulls and Common Terns at Snettisham, then spend the evening on a nearby heathland listening to the churring of Nightjars and roding Woodcocks.

West Norfolk is a fine place to watch autumn bird migration, when flocks of thrushes fly along the coastline of the Wash. Snettisham and Hunstanton are good locations to witness this remarkable phenomenon.

# 1.01 Hunstanton

Spectacular cliffs that are a Fulmar breeding site and provide a vantage point for viewing seabirds.

## Birds
Year round: Fulmar
Autumn: visible migration
Winter: sea ducks, divers, grebes, Purple Sandpiper

## Location (Car park, lighthouse, TF677422, beach car park TF681425, jet-ski ramp TF668399)
Turn west off the A149 onto Lighthouse Lane, the B1161, and follow to the lighthouse and car park on the right.

## Opening times and access
Access is on foot only. There is a pay and display car park at the lighthouse or park along the B1161. The beach car park (for scrub areas) costs £2.

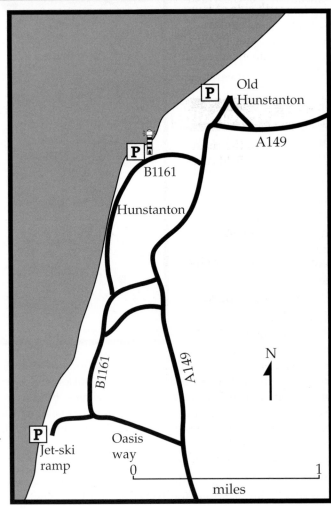

## Other amenities
All available in Hunstanton.

## Birdwatching tips
Fulmars can readily be seen from the cliff tops south of the lighthouse as they
wheel by. Scouring the sea from here for divers and grebes will require a telescope
as the birds tend to be rather far offshore. Strong onshore winds, preferably north-
easterlies, are necessary for good seabird passage in late summer to autumn.
Visible migration, particularly of larks and thrushes, is best in light winds with a
northerly component in the late autumn. The mile walk north from Hunstanton to
Holme can be good for migrants any time there are classic fall conditions – north-
easterly or easterly winds, preferably with drizzle, mist or rain. Park at the beach
car park, make your way to the coast and walk north-east following the cliff top.
Purple Sandpipers are occasionally seen on the rocks at the base of the cliffs. To
access the seafront, take the track through the dunes from the lighthouse car park
and walk south.

At the south side of Hunstanton is a jet-ski ramp where Purple Sandpipers and
other waders regularly roost at high tide. To reach this site, turn west off the A149
at the south side of Hunstanton onto Oasis Way, the B1161. Go straight on at the
next roundabout, then at the next junction, turn left onto South Beach Road. Park
after 50 yards. On your right is the jet-ski ramp.

# 1.02 Heacham

Easy access to the coast along the west side of the Wash. Inland the rough
grassland and fields can prove productive for migrants, especially in the spring.

## Birds
Year round: gulls
Spring: Wheatear,
migrants
Winter: Purple Sandpiper

## Location (Car park
TF664377)
From the north, take the
B1161 roundabout at the
south end of Hunstanton,
turn west towards the
coast along South Beach

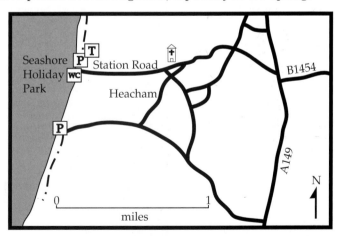

Road. At the sharp right-hand bend, turn left (still on South Beach Road) and keep
following it up over a concrete ramp. The tarmac soon runs out and the road
becomes a track. On the left is a raised bank that allows viewing over some rough
grassy fields and later a golf course. On the right are private holiday huts which
prevent access to the beach but after about a mile there is a turning to a caravan
park to the left and opposite you can park and walk to the beach.

Approaching from the south, turn west into Heacham off the A149 just north of the B1454 turning to Sedgeford. Just after passing the Methodist church, bear right, signposted to North Beach, along Station Road. 1.5 miles from the A149, you reach a roundabout. Turn right to the car park. Park here and walk to the shore.

## Opening times and access
There is open access on foot, but the area is mainly private. The car park is pay and display.

## Other amenities
There is a chip shop along Station Road. Other facilities can be found in Heacham or Hunstanton.

## Birdwatching tips
Check the sea groynes for Purple Sandpipers, particularly in the winter. Gulls are to be found all the way along the shore, but note that this is a popular place and therefore the birds are frequently disturbed. As you drive/walk along the rough track between Hunstanton and Heacham, stop wherever you can and climb the bank to the east to check the grassy areas for migrants.

# 1.03 Snettisham

An RSPB nature reserve on the west Norfolk coast that is famous for its large numbers of waders and Pink-footed Geese.

## Birds
Spring: Waders, early migrants
Summer: Waders, including Avocet, gulls, terns
Autumn: Greenshank, Spotted Redshank, Little Stint, Curlew Sandpiper, Knot
Winter: Pink-footed Goose, Red-breasted Merganser, Goldeneye, Kingfisher, large numbers of Knot

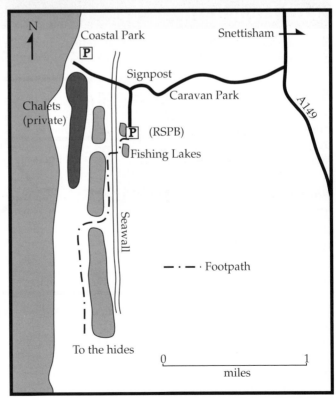

## Location (Car park TF650329)

RSPB Snettisham is signposted to the west off the A149 between Dersingham and Snettisham. After 1.5 miles, where the road bears right, turn left signposted to the RSPB/KLAA car park and follow the signposted walk.

## Management

RSPB nature reserve.

## Opening times and access

Open access on foot. Disabled visitors should phone the reserve office on 01485 542689 for help with access. There is a gate which may be locked overnight. If so, times are indicated on it when it will be opened. Car parking is free to RSPB members and costs £2 for non-members. There are four hides plus a special hide that is ideal for photographing high-tide wader roosts, which can be hired through the reserve office.

## Other amenities

A shop just beyond the car park sells basic supplies in summer. Nearby Snettisham village has numerous other amenities.

## Birdwatching tips

Snettisham is famous for its high-tide wader roost. To witness this spectacle, you need to visit on a day with a big high tide. The RSPB has produced birdwatchers' tide tables to highlight these occasions. These are available from the Snettisham office (01485 542689) and from the Titchwell RSPB shop (01485 210779), price 50p. You need to be on site about 1.5 hours before high-tide to see the most impressive wader flights.

Internationally-important numbers of Pink-footed Geese are present from late October to early February. They are unpredictable in their habits, but to maximise your chances of witnessing the dawn flight of geese from the Wash inland to their feeding grounds, you should avoid visiting 3–4 days either side of a full moon; at these times the geese stay feeding out in the fields late and do not fly out again in spectacular movements at dawn. The coastal park and area around the coastal pay and display car park is worth exploring during migration periods.

# 1.04 Dersingham Bog (a) and Wolferton (b)

Dersingham Bog is a small nature reserve within the Sandringham Royal Estate that protects an area of acid valley mire, heathland and woodland. There is a boardwalk that allows safe viewing of the remarkable acid bog. The minor roads here and the A149 form a triangle that is a noted site for seeing Golden Pheasants.

## Birds

Winter and spring: Golden Pheasant
Summer: Nightjar, Long-eared Owl, Crossbill

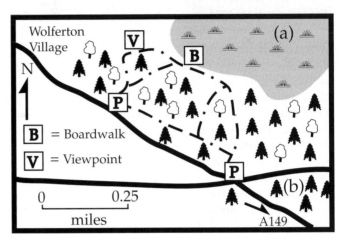

## Location (Car park TF668280)

Turn west off the A149 about 4 miles north of King's Lynn onto the minor road signposted to Wolferton. Park on the right after about half a mile, on the northern arm of the scissors crossroads. Go through the gate and follow the walking trail through the wood until you reach an open area and then the boardwalk on your right. The "Golden Pheasant" triangle is formed by the A149 and the two minor roads that lead west off it signposted to Wolferton, at TF673277 and TF674280. Alternatively (especially useful for dusk visits to see Nightjars), carry along the northern arm to a car park on the right at TF662285. Follow the signs to the sea cliff and head down the hill to the boardwalk.

## Management

English Nature. The Site Manager can be contacted through the English Nature Norwich Office, 60 Bracondale, Norwich NR21 2BE, tel. 01603 620558.

## Opening times and access

Car parking space is very limited. Public access is on foot only on wide well-maintained walking tracks. This is a sensitive area so keep strictly to the footpaths. Free leaflets are available at the car parks and along the boardwalk.

## Other amenities

All readily available nearby in King's Lynn.

## Birdwatching tips

The best strategy to see Golden Pheasants is to wait for birds to cross the minor roads that form two sides of the Wolferton triangle. Birds regularly cross at dawn and the best chance of success seems to be in winter or early spring when the roads are quieter. A good technique is to listen for calling birds and then pull off and wait in your car until a pheasant crosses over in front of you.

Dersingham Bog is one of the best sites in Norfolk for seeing Nightjars. Try to visit on a warm, still evening in late May through to early July and wait at the edge of the cleared area near the bog. You should hear birds churring and see them hunting over the cleared area, sometimes before it is even fully dark.

## 1.05 Flitcham and Abbey Farm

Flitcham has a grazing marsh and small pools that host a variety of farmland birds. Abbey Farm is run in an environmentally-sensitive manner and bags of bird feed mix grown on the farm are sold there.

### Birds
Year round: Egyptian Goose, Little and Barn Owls, Tree Sparrow
Autumn and winter: Pink-footed Goose, raptors including Red Kite (best Oct–Nov), Common Buzzard, Water Rail, Kingfisher

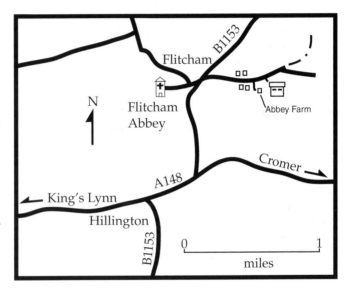

### Location (Car park TF737265)
At the A149/A148 roundabout north-east of King's Lynn, take the A148 north-east to Cromer. After about 3 miles, shortly after the village of Hillington, turn left onto the B1153 and take the first right-hand turn in the village of Flitcham – after half a mile look out for a sign on your right to the birdwatchers hide. Park in the small car park and follow signs to the hide, which is about 40 yards from the car park and is fully accessible to wheelchair users. Flitcham is on a bus route from King's Lynn. There is open foot access to pastureland to the east and west of the hide: details are posted in the hide.

### Management
A privately tenanted farm on the Sandringham Estate.

### Opening times and access
Car parking is free and access is on foot only to the hide, during daylight.

### Other amenities
There is a public phone in Flitcham and there are garages along the A148.

## Birdwatching tips

The old oak tree in front of the hide regularly has Little Owls sitting in it, particularly at dusk. Pink-footed Geese feed on the aftermath of the sugar beet crop on fields in this area. These birds are highly sensitive to disturbance and are extremely wary. If you are lucky enough to find a flock close to a road, do not get out of your car as this will certainly flush them.

# 1.06 Fishers Fleet (a) and Lynn Point (b)

Fishers Fleet is one of the premier sites for gulls in Norfolk. Lynn Point, where the River Great Ouse joins the Wash, can also be very good.

## Birds

Year round: gulls, waders
Summer: Marsh Harrier, Yellow-legged Gull
Winter: Brent Goose, Glaucous Gull

## Location (Car park, Fishers Fleet, TF615208, Lynn Point, TF605231)

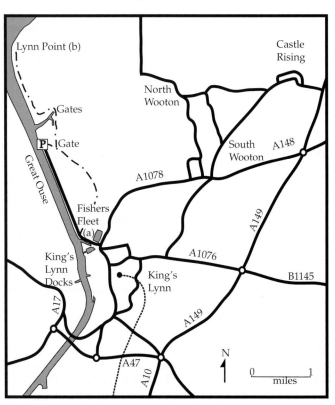

From the A148/A149 roundabout north-east of King's Lynn, turn south-west on the A148 towards King's Lynn, signposted to the "Docks" and "South Wooton". At the traffic lights at the A148/A1078 junction, carry straight on along the A1078. Carry straight on at the next set of traffic lights and then turn right at a sharp left-hand bend (4.3 miles from the A149 roundabout), cross the railway line and carry on for 0.4 miles until you see the Fishers Fleet creek on your left. Park here. To reach Lynn Point, carry on along this road (ignoring the Dow Chemical factory turning a further 0.3 miles on) which becomes a rough track for a further 1.5 miles. Park by the sharp right-hand bend just before a gate blocks your way. Walk round the side of the gate, then after a short distance, follow the seawall off to the north. Just after crossing over the sluice, go over a stile by the next gate then turn immediately left through another gate and follow the seawall to the coast. Lynn Point is reached after about 1.5 miles. You can either view the geese from this seawall or at other times of the year it is possible to walk across the saltmarsh to view the muddy edges of the River Great Ouse. It is possible to follow this seawall all the way along the coast to Heacham.

## Opening times and access

Open access on foot, although some hunting takes place in the Lynn Point area and access may not be possible at such times.

## Other amenities

All available in King's Lynn.

## Birdwatching tips

The channel at Fishers Fleet allows excellent views from the road of both large and small gulls. They should be scrutinised for both regular Yellow-legged Gulls (summer months best) and Glaucous Gulls (winter best). Many gulls congregate on the River Great Ouse of which Fishers Fleet is an offshoot. Check the birds on the water with a telescope from the road that runs alongside the channel. Gulls and waders are found along the muddy sides of the River Great Ouse and in winter Brent Geese are on the saltmarsh. Try to visit at high tide when birds will be pushed off the extensive mudflats of the Wash. Lynn Point can be good after strong northerly gales, especially in the late summer/autumn. At such times seabirds, including skuas, are sometimes pushed right into the mouth of the River Great Ouse.

# 1.07 Roydon Common

A good place to find commoner heathland species. At all times keep to the marked footpath to avoid disturbing breeding birds.

## Birds

Year round: Green Woodpecker
Spring and summer: Nightjar, Nightingale, Woodcock, Tree Pipit, Woodlark

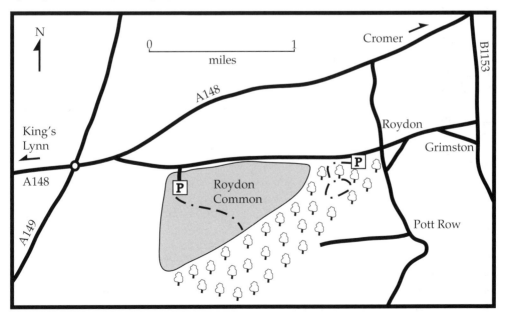

## Location (Car park, west end TF678226, east end TF697228)

From the A148/A149 roundabout just north-east of King's Lynn, head north-east on the A148 towards Fakenham. After 0.2 miles, turn right, signposted to Grimston. For the western end, turn south after 0.6 miles onto a rough track, passing an open area on the left-hand side. Park after 0.3 miles and take the footpath east across the open heath until you reach a gate and the edge of the pine forest after about 0.5 miles. For the eastern end, from the A148 Grimston road turning, drive east for 0.9 miles then turn south into the signposted car park. Coming from the east, this is 0.2 miles west of the Pott Row turning.

## Management

Norfolk Wildlife Trust. For a leaflet to accompany your walk, tel. 01603 625540.

## Opening times and access

Open access on foot at all times.

## Other amenities

All readily available in King's Lynn.

## Birdwatching tips

The western access point is an excellent place to see Nightjars because the open heathland allows views over a wide area. Try to visit at dusk on a calm, warm summer evening and pick a suitable vantage point along the footpath. Anywhere around the car park at the eastern end is a good place to hear Nightingales. An evening visit on a calm warm spring or summer day is recommended.

# 1.08 Massingham Heath

An area of rough open grassland that in recent winters has been a favoured haunt of Rough-legged Buzzards. Visitors must keep strictly to public rights of way and footpaths when accessing this sensitive site.

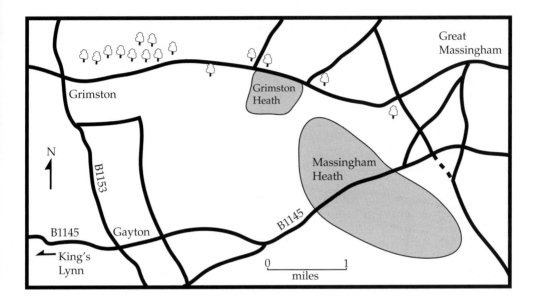

## Birds
Winter: Rough-legged Buzzard

## Location (Car park; there is limited parking at TF791211)
Massingham Heath is about 7 miles east of King's Lynn, and much of it is most easily covered from the B1145, east of Gayton.

## Opening times and access
Privately owned land with no public access other than along public rights of way.

## Other amenities
All readily available in nearby King's Lynn.

## Birdwatching tips
Easiest to cover by car, pulling off and scanning for raptors wherever possible. The B1145 cuts right through Massingham Heath and this is a good place to start. Try to visit on calm, sunny days in the winter for the best chance of finding a Rough-legged Buzzard. A good track to walk is the section of the Peddars Way and Norfolk Coast Path between the B1145 at TF791211 south-east to where it joins up with the minor road south of Great Massingham at TF795201.

# 1.09 Pentney Gravel Pits

A working gravel pit in west Norfolk that attracts passage waders and wildfowl, including breeding Egyptian Geese. Gulls foraging on the nearby Blackborough rubbish tip (where viewing is extremely limited) regularly visit the pits at Pentney to wash and preen, often allowing excellent views. The nearby Pentney Lakes Leisure Park is generally too disturbed for birds. The easternmost lake, however, does have some good wader habitat. It is easily covered from the minor road west of Pentney at TF716134.

## Birds
Year round: Egyptian Goose
Spring and autumn: waders, gulls
Winter: wildfowl, gulls

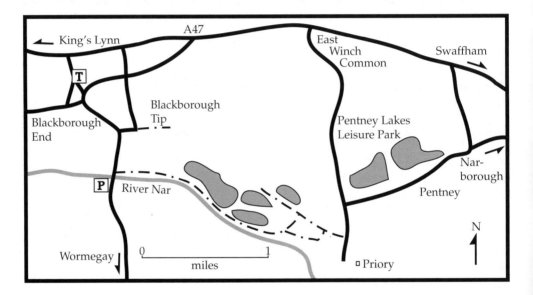

## Location (Car park TF670136)
Situated about 5 miles south-east of King's Lynn, park at High Bridge on the minor road between Blackborough and Wormegay and take the track east along the north side of the River Nar. This track gives excellent views over a series of pits, mainly to the north.

## Management
A privately owned and managed working gravel pit. Please keep strictly to the wide well-maintained access tracks.

## Opening times and access
There is limited parking at High Bridge. Access is on foot only.

## Other amenities
All readily available in nearby King's Lynn.

## Birdwatching tips
The first pit on the left, reached after about half a mile, is often favoured by gulls from the Blackborough rubbish tip. Waders favour any muddy margins and the small islands in the pits, and wildfowl are on any of the open areas of water.

Just east of Pentney, the Mill at nearby Narborough (TF746131) is a breeding site for Grey Wagtail, a scarce bird in Norfolk. East Winch Common, a small reserve located off the minor road that runs south from the A149 towards Pentney Lakes Leisure Park (TF700158), is a good site for both Marsh and Willow Tits.

# 1.10 Tottenhill Gravel Pits

A privately owned site with limited viewing from public roads. It is a regular wintering site for Smew.

## Birds
Summer: Nightingale
Winter: Smew

## Location (Limited viewing at TF632113)
Turn west off the A10 5 miles south of King's Lynn by the crossroads at the Dray and Horses pub at TF637111, just south of the A10/A134 junction. Stop after about half a mile where you can see the main pit on your right. There is a second pit, less attractive to birds, between the A10 and the A134. Turn south-east off the A10 onto the

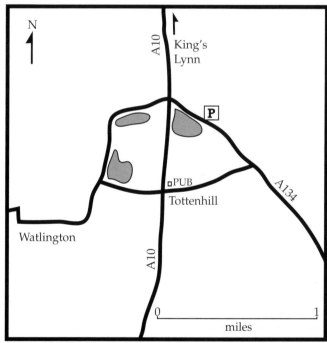

A134 and stop on the left after 0.3 miles. Walk back to where you can view a large pit to the west, through the trees. At both sites there is limited car parking. Park carefully and safely.

## Opening times and access
*On no account enter this private property – view only from public roads.*

### Other amenities
The Dray and Horse pub is located next to the A10, close to this site. Other amenities are available in nearby King's Lynn.

### Birdwatching tips
Nightingales occur in the thick hedgerows surrounding the main pit in summer.

# 1.11 Welney

A superb Wildfowl & Wetlands Trust (WWT) site that holds birds at all times of the year, but is perhaps most famous for the large numbers of wildfowl that visit in winter. The heated hide makes close viewing of migrant wildfowl a pure delight during the winter.

### Birds
Year round: wildfowl
Spring, summer and autumn: Garganey, waders, terns, warblers, Marsh Harrier, Avocet
Winter: Bewick's and Whooper Swans

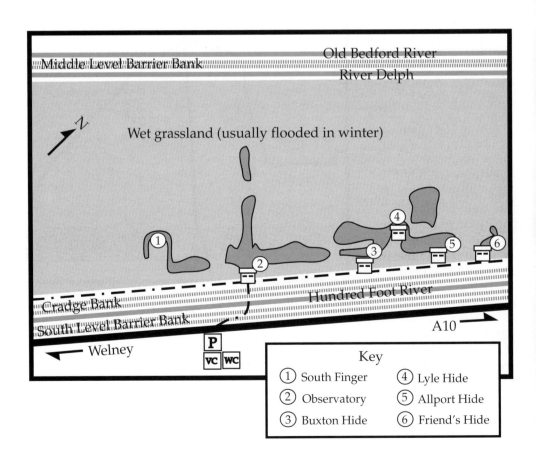

## Location (Car park TL547945)

WWT Welney is situated 12 miles north of Ely. It is signposted from the A10 between Downham Market and Ely and the A1101. The road between Welney village (on the A1101) and the centre sometimes floods during the winter. Access is always possible from the A10. You will need to visit the visitor centre to get a permit to visit the hides, which are a short distance away on the opposite side of the road.

## Management

Wildfowl & Wetlands Trust nature reserve.

## Opening times and access

The reserve is open 10 am to 5 pm daily, except Christmas Day. The Reception Centre is open until 8 pm on Wednesday–Sunday from mid-November until the end of February. Car parking is free. Permits, available from the Reception Centre, cost £3.50 for adults, £2 for children aged 4 to 16, £2.75 for single parents or the unwaged or £9 for families. Entrance is free to WWT members. Access is by foot only to the six hides. The Reception Centre has toilets, a gift and book shop and sells hot snacks and drinks. Binoculars can be hired for £1 and wheelchairs are available for loan (no charge).

## Other amenities

These are available in nearby Welney village.

## Birdwatching tips

There is a noticeboard with recent bird sightings at the Reception Centre. Spend time in the various hides and carefully scrutinise the large waterbird flocks. American Wigeons are fairly regular here, and in the winters of 1996/7 and 1997/8 a male Canvasback associated with the Pochard flock. The hides are all accessible along the 0.5 mile Screenbank Walk. There is also a longer (2.5 miles) Summer Walk and a short Reedbed Boardwalk to the small reedbed. In the winter the site sometimes becomes flooded so that access is only possible to the main Observatory Hide. At these times there is a reduced admission fee.

# 1.12 Ouse Washes

Although in Cambridgeshire, the Ouse Washes are contiguous with the fen country of west Norfolk and Welney. It is a superb birding site and with 10 hides and more than 1,000 ha of wet grassland to investigate, you could easily stay an entire day.

## Birds

Spring and summer: Garganey, waders (including up to 1,500–2,000 Icelandic race Black-tailed Godwits during their peak passage in March/April) and wildfowl, Tree Sparrow, Corn Bunting
Autumn: waders
Winter: wildfowl (including Bewick's and Whooper Swans), gulls, Tree Sparrow, Corn Bunting

## Location (Car park TL470859)

The RSPB nature reserve is about 7 miles north of Ely, and the car park is 2.5 miles from Manea off the A142 from Ely along Park Road. Turn opposite the Rose and Crown pub signposted to "Purls Bridge and Welches Dam RSPB Reserve".

## Management

Managed by the RSPB but jointly owned by them and the Cambridgeshire Wildlife Trust.

## Opening times and access

The car park is free and the hides are always open. The visitor centre is open daily from 9 am to 5 pm, except Christmas Day and New Year's Day. There are 10 hides, with wheelchair access to Welches Dam hide from the visitor centre car park; otherwise access is on foot only.

## Other amenities

There are toilets on site, the Ship Inn at Purls Bridge sells food and other amenities are all readily available in nearby Chatteris.

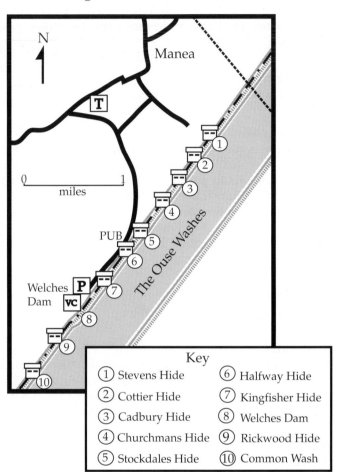

**Key**

| | |
|---|---|
| ① Stevens Hide | ⑥ Halfway Hide |
| ② Cottier Hide | ⑦ Kingfisher Hide |
| ③ Cadbury Hide | ⑧ Welches Dam |
| ④ Churchmans Hide | ⑨ Rickwood Hide |
| ⑤ Stockdales Hide | ⑩ Common Wash |

## Birdwatching tips

To cover this site fully, you should ideally spend time in all 10 hides. An afternoon or evening visit is recommended as otherwise you will be looking from the hides straight into the sun. This is also the best time of the day to view the large gull roost that forms in the winter. Get there early enough to find out where the birds are currently gathering or ask for up-to-date information in the visitor centre. Tree Sparrows and Corn Buntings are resident but perhaps most easily seen in winter when the RSPB puts out food for them near the visitor centre. Tree Sparrow nest boxes have recently been built here. Wildfowling occurs on privately-owned areas, some of which are overlooked from the hides. During the wildfowling season (1 October to 31 January), most disturbance occurs on Saturdays. There is no wildfowling on Sundays.

# Chapter 2: North Norfolk

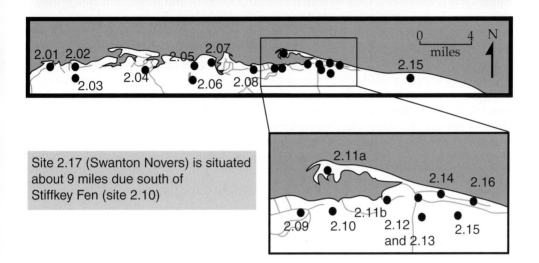

Site 2.17 (Swanton Novers) is situated about 9 miles due south of Stiffkey Fen (site 2.10)

## Introduction

North Norfolk is probably the most famous birdwatching area in the UK. A series of nature reserves stretches along the coast from Holme in the west to Cley in the east, protecting a network of coastal grazing marshes and lagoons, home to many exciting breeding species and migrants. The long shingle spit of Blakeney Point is famous for attracting migrant passerines, especially during autumn. This very special landscape has been designated an Area of Outstanding Natural Beauty, a Site of Special Scientific Interest, a Special Protection Area, a Ramsar site and a Special Area of Conservation.

## Special birds

The coastal reedbeds are home to breeding Marsh Harriers, Bearded Tits, the occasional pair of Bitterns and in winter to roosting Hen Harriers. North Norfolk's extensive grazing marshes support large numbers of wintering wildfowl, including flocks of Brent, Pink-footed and White-fronted Geese. At this season the beaches are some of the UK's most reliable wintering sites for Shorelarks. In summer, the heathlands host breeding Nightjars and Nightingales. The whole area is rightly famous for rare and exciting migrants and a year never passes by without several rarities being sighted.

## Timing

Birdwatching on the north Norfolk coast can be excellent at any time of the year. Avocets return to Titchwell in mid-February, a month later the first Wheatears and Chiffchaffs can be found. Spring migration picks up in April and by the month's end the coastal reedbeds resound to the songs of warblers. In late April, Marsh Harriers perform their sky-dancing display flights over the reedbeds at Titchwell and Cley. May is the classic spring month to visit the coast, when many breeding species have already arrived, many spring migrants are present alongside the last winter birds, and there is always the chance of finding a rare migrant.

Summer is a wonderful time to watch breeding Avocets and terns, and this is also the time to look for night birds and to listen for Nightjars churring at dusk. Autumn starts early, and by mid-July the first returning waders appear. Numbers build up during July and August but gradually dwindle thereafter. During September and October the last of the summer migrants have departed to be replaced by winter wildfowl and thrushes. These months are when birdwatchers pray for easterly winds for these bring migrant passerines, which always include some far-eastern gems. Pallas's and Yellow-browed Warblers are both annual, and there is always the chance of finding an extreme rarity. This is a wonderful time to watch the arrival of flocks of thrushes and other diurnal migrants, and the coastal reedbeds resound to the calls of erupting Bearded Tits.

Winter is the time to watch flocks of Pink-footed Geese freshly arrived from Iceland, while at Holkham you can find feeding flocks of Snow Buntings, Twites and Shorelarks. Barn Owls can often be seen hunting in daylight, and a dusk vigil at Titchwell may be rewarded with the sight of a Hen Harrier drifting into its roost site in the reedbed.

## Safety on the coast

The north Norfolk coast is a wild place; for your own safety it is important that you keep to public rights of way and do not venture out onto the saltmarshes where you may be easily cut off by the incoming tide.

# 2.01 Holme NOA (a) and NWT (b) reserves

Holme Dunes National Nature Reserve is famous as a migration watchpoint, and more than 300 species have been recorded in the area. Two organistions run reserves at Holme: the Norfolk Wildlife Trust (NWT) and Norfolk Ornithologists Association (NOA). South-easterly winds are best in the spring, north-east winds best in the autumn for scarce migrants. The best conditions for visible migration in the autumn are when the winds are between the south-east and south-west and there is a light cloud cover. At such times flocks of birds hug the east coast, so they are not pushed out to sea by the offshore winds, while the cloud cover keeps them low enough to be easily seen. Strong north-westerlies are best for seawatching.

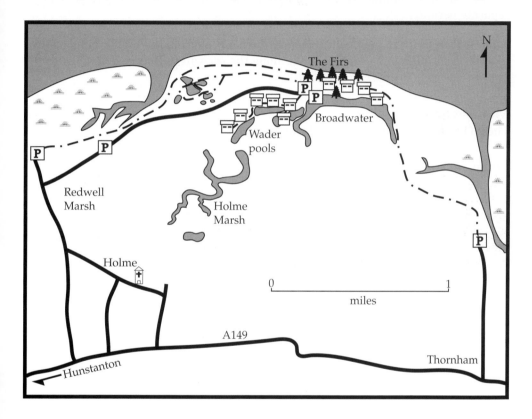

## Birds
Year round: Barn and Tawny Owls
Spring: early migrants including Swallow, Wheatear, Cuckoo and warblers
Summer: Avocet, Grasshopper Warbler
Autumn: migrant warblers and thrushes, visible migration, rarities
Winter: ducks, geese, Hen Harrier, Short-eared Owl, Shorelark

## Other amenities
The White Horse pub in Holme village serves meals and there is a public phone nearby. Other amenities are readily available in nearby Hunstanton.

## 2.01(a) Holme NOA Reserve

### Location (Car park TF715449)

The NOA reserve is signposted from the A149 coast road. From Hunstanton, take the first left turn (TF700429, signposted), drive to the end of this road and turn right just before the toilet block by the golf course, along a rutted dirt track and follow to the NOA reserve and car park on the right hand side (with the shrike logo). This track passes over the NWT's Holme Dunes reserve, but if you are only visiting the NOA observatory, you do not require an NWT permit. Go to the NOA reception to obtain a permit. There is a small hut here where drinks and sweets can be bought in summer. If you also wish to visit the NWT reserve, you must get a separate permit.

Alternatively you can park at Thornham Harbour (park on the high ground as the road floods at high tide), and walk out along the seawall to Holme. You will still require a permit to enter the reserve.

### Management

The NOA has a 5.3 ha reserve and ringing station.

### Opening times and access

The NOA reserve is open to members from dawn to dusk daily, but otherwise the reserves and access road are open from 10 am to 5 pm daily, although there is access along the public right of way that skirts the edge of the dunes at all times. Special openings are usually arranged if there is a rarity in the area. NOA members receive free access to the reserve and use of the seawatching hide. The NOA reserve has four hides; one overlooks Broadwater, one is a seawatching hide and there are two hides in the scrub that face north. The NOA has built a hide at Redwell Marsh. The nearest public toilet is in Holme village by the golf course.

### Birdwatching tips

From the NOA car park, take the path to the rear of the house through the five-bar gate with Broadwater on your right. Follow the track to the observatory. Check all areas of scrub for passage migrants, which sometimes include exciting rarities.

## 2.01(b) Holme NWT Reserve

### Location (Car park TF715449)

Holme NWT reserve is signposted from the A149 coast road. From Hunstanton take the first left turn (TF700429), drive to the end of this road and turn right (signposted) just before the toilet block by the golf course, along a rutted dirt track. There may be a hut open where you will have to pay to visit the NWT reserve at this point. At the end of the track, park in the car park in front of the white house and obtain a permit for the NWT reserve from the visitor centre. Note you must get separate permits for NWT and NOA.

Alternatively it is possible to park at Thornham Harbour (park on the high ground as the road floods at high tide) and walk out along the seawall to Holme.

### Management

The reserve is managed by the Norfolk Wildlife Trust.

### Opening times and access

The access road is open from 10 am to 5 pm daily, although there is access along the public right of way that skirts the edge of the dunes at all times. Special openings are usually arranged if there is a rarity in the area. There are four old hides on the NWT reserve and a marked trail through the "Firs". The NWT visitor centre sells drinks and sweets, but has no toilets.

### Birdwatching tips

The area around the first car park can be good for Grasshopper Warblers in spring/ early summer. Park in the first car park and walk back along the edge of the scrub overlooking The Paddocks, which can be good in the early morning for migrant warblers and thrushes. From here drive or walk to the visitor centre and collect your NWT permit.

Keeping to marked paths, explore the area of sea buckthorn known as "The Firs". In autumn this area regularly holds birds like Yellow-browed and Pallas's Warblers. The Pine trees behind the visitor centre are worth a look and can hold migrant chats, warblers and crests.

### Non-bird interest

In spring and early summer, listen for Natterjack Toads. These can be seen during summer on the patio of the Lifeboat pub in Thornham. They emerge at dusk from underneath the paving slabs and scurry about between drinkers' feet!

# 2.02 Titchwell Marsh

Titchwell is the most visited RSPB nature reserve. Its diverse range of habitats can all be easily explored within a short walk from the car park. Habitats include woodland, reedfen, reedbed, freshwater and brackish lagoons, saltmarsh, beach and sea. The reserve has attracted a mouth-watering selection of rarities, including Ross's, Laughing and Franklin's Gulls, Collared and Black-winged Pratincoles, Penduline Tit and Surf Scoter. A Black-winged Stilt has been resident at the reserve for several years.

## Birds

Year round: Black-winged Stilt, Mediterranean Gull, Barn Owl, Sparrowhawk, Water Rail, Bearded Tit, Bullfinch, Little Egrets are increasingly present throughout the year
Spring: Avocet (from mid-February), Marsh Harrier, Garganey, Blackcap, Chiffchaff, Whitethroat, Lesser Whitethroat, Garden, Willow, Reed and Sedge Warblers
Summer: Common, Sandwich and Little Terns, warblers, Marsh Harrier, Avocet
Autumn: Up to 30 species of waders. Little Stint and Curlew Sandpiper sometimes in large flocks
Winter: Shorelark, Rock Pipit, Twite, Linnet, Snow Bunting, Common and Velvet Scoters, Slavonian Grebe, Red-throated Diver, Long-tailed Duck, Hen Harrier, Merlin, Peregrine, Short-eared Owl

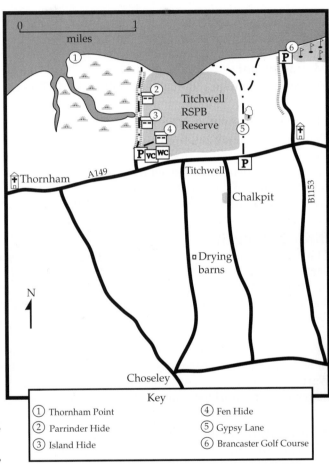

Key
① Thornham Point
② Parrinder Hide
③ Island Hide
④ Fen Hide
⑤ Gypsy Lane
⑥ Brancaster Golf Course

## Location (Car park TF750438)

The reserve is signposted from the A149 coast road six miles east of Hunstanton between the villages of Thornham and Titchwell. The reserve is served by the Coastliner bus service (tel. 0845 3006116) and has its own request bus stop. There are cycle racks by the visitor centre.

## Management
Managed by the RSPB.

## Opening times and access
The reserve and its three hides are open at all times. Dogs are allowed on the
West Bank path but are not allowed on the Fen and Meadow Nature Trails or in
the hides (guide dogs excepted). There is no permit fee; however, RSPB members
should leave their membership card on their car dashboard and non-members
should pay to park (£3 per vehicle in 2001). There are toilets (including disabled)
in the car park. The visitor centre is open daily, except Christmas and Boxing
Days. It has a shop with a good range of books and optics, with binoculars
available for hire, and sells hot and cold snacks. Recent sightings are displayed on
a board outside the centre and on another over the information desk. For an up-
to-date events leaflet send a SAE to Titchwell Marsh RSPB reserve, Titchwell,
Norfolk PE31 8BB or call 01485 210779 for further information.

## Other amenities
Pubs and hotels in the nearby villages all serve food. There are public phones in
Thornham and Brancaster. The nearest garages are in Hunstanton and Burnham
Deepdale.

## Birdwatching tips
The West Bank path runs south to north from the visitor centre to the sea, with
the main scrape and fen to the east of the track. Evening is therefore best, with
the setting sun behind you. The Fen and Meadow Trails are excellent for warblers
in summer. Check the bird feeder at the back of the visitor centre, especially in
winter, when you may see Siskin, Brambling, Tree Sparrow, Redpoll and Great
Spotted Woodpecker. Bearded Tits are easiest to see from mid-July to the end of
September when, on still calm mornings, flocks can be seen in the reeds beside
the West Bank path and around the bridge to the Island Hide. Little Egret
numbers start to build up in late summer. This reserve is very popular,
particularly at weekends and bank holidays, when the car park is often full.

## Non-bird interest
Water Voles are found in the reedbed dikes. There have been sightings of Otters in
recent years, Common Seals can be seen offshore and the new dragonfly pool is
worth looking at in late summer. The Meadow Trail in spring is good for Marsh
Orchid and Ragged Robin.

# 2.03 Choseley Area

An area of private farmland intersected by roads and public footpaths.

## Birds
Year round: Grey Partridge, Barn and Little Owls, Tree Sparrow, Corn Bunting, Yellowhammer
Summer: Quail

## Location (TF 758421)
The area is just inland from Titchwell, on the north Norfolk coast (see the Titchwell map (2.02) for the location of Choseley). Turn south off the A149 by the Titchwell village sign (the first turning on the right coming from the west). After 1 mile, park sensibly by the farm barns, ensuring that you are not blocking any gateways.

## Management
Privately owned working farm.

## Opening times and access
Viewing is from public roads and footpaths.

## Other amenities
There are public phones in Thornham and Brancaster, a garage in Burnham Deepdale, and pubs and hotels on the A149 coast road.

## Birdwatching tips
Do not wander near the barns, but stand and wait for birds to feed on spilled grain around them. Quails are sometimes present in summer. Walk the footpath along the ridge top that runs from east to west, away from the barns. You are unlikely to see any Quails, but have a good chance of hearing them. Do not tresspass onto the fields under any circumstances.

# 2.04 Burnham Norton

An English Nature managed grazing marsh with shallow floods and reed-fringed ditches.

## Birds

Year round: Barn Owl
Spring and summer: Avocet, Redshank, Lapwing and Oystercatcher, Reed and Sedge Warblers
Autumn: wildfowl and migrants
Winter: Brent and Pink-footed Geese

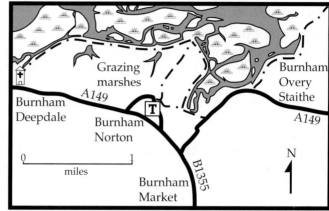

## Location (Car park TF 828441)

Burnham Norton is signposted off the A149 between Burnham Deepdale and Burnham Overy Staithe. The car park is on the east side of the road on a sharp bend. Please do not park in the village.

## Management

English Nature Reserve.

## Opening times and access

Public rights of way circle the reserve.

## Other amenities

There is a phone on the east side of the village. The nearest garage is in Burnham Deepdale. There are pubs in Burnham Deepdale and Burnham Overy Staithe.

## Birdwatching tips

Follow the circular walk from the car park at the north end of the village. From the sea wall, head west for a short way to overlook some reed-fringed pools. Dusk in the winter is a good time to watch from the car park for the resident Barn Owls.

# 2.05 Holkham

## 2.05(a) Grazing Marsh and Lady Anne's Drive

## 2.05(b) Holkham Bay

## 2.05(c) The Pines and Wells Wood

This excellent birdwatching area covers a range of habitats and is treated in three sections. Holkham Hall is covered as a separate site (2.06).

## 2.05a Grazing Marsh and Lady Anne's Drive

### Birds

Spring and summer: Lapwing, Redshank, Snipe, Marsh Harrier, wildfowl
Autumn: returning wildfowl
Winter: Pink-footed, Brent (including regular Black Brants and Pale-bellied), White-fronted, Egyptian, Canada, Greylag and occasional Bean Geese, Wigeon, Hen Harrier

### Location (Car park TF 891448)

Turn off the A149 into Lady Anne's Drive between Burnham Overy Staithe and Wells, about 1 mile west of the latter. The turning is opposite the turn to Holkham Hall (site 2.06), by the Victoria pub, at TF892440.

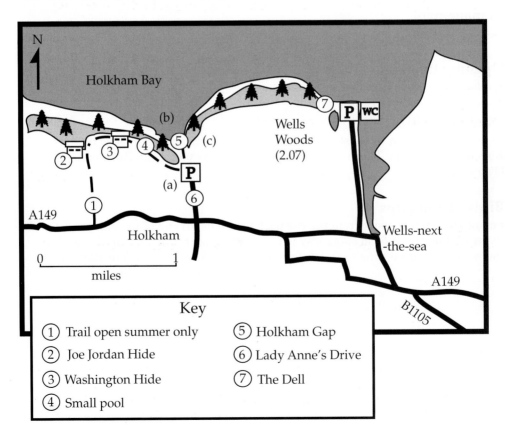

N

Holkham Bay

(b)

Wells
Woods
(2.07)

7  P  WC

(c)

5

4

2  3

P
(a)

6

A149

1

Holkham

Wells-next
-the-sea

0          1

miles

A149

B1105

### Key

(1) Trail open summer only      (5) Holkham Gap
(2) Joe Jordan Hide             (6) Lady Anne's Drive
(3) Washington Hide            (7) The Dell
(4) Small pool

## Management
An English Nature National Nature Reserve managed in association with the Holkham Estate.

## Opening times and access
Open access at all times. There is a car parking fee of £2 for Lady Anne's Drive. There are two hides in the pines overlooking the grazing marshes and the Washington Hide has disabled access.

## Other amenities
The Victoria pub by the turning off the main road serves food and provides accommodation. The nearest phone is just east of the Holkham turning on the A149. Other amenities are all readily available in nearby Wells.

## Birdwatching tips
This is the best place in Norfolk to watch wild geese. Scope the birds from Lady Anne's Drive or walk east or west along the footpaths that skirt the northern edge of the grazing marsh.

## 2.05(b) Holkham Bay & 2.05(c) Holkham Pines
This belt of pines is one of the best places to search for wind-blown vagrants in the autumn. In the winter the bay is perhaps the best place in Norfolk to look for Shorelark, Snow Bunting and Twite. The eastern end of the woods is treated separately as Wells Woods (2.07).

## Birds
Spring and autumn: migrants, including Goldcrest and regular Yellow-browed and Pallas's Warblers in autumn
Winter: Shorelark, Twite, Snow and Lapland Buntings

## Location
Access is from Lady Anne's Drive (see above) or Wells Beach car park (TF913455). A fee is payable at both car parks.

## Management
This is part of the English Nature Holkham National Nature Reserve.

## Opening times and access
There is free public access at all times and a viewing platform that overlooks Holkham Bay.

## Birdwatching tips
From the car park at the end of Lady Anne's Drive, walk through the belt of pine trees and onto a boardwalk that takes you to a viewing platform overlooking the bay. This is the best place from which to locate the mixed winter flock of Shorelarks, Twites, Snow Buntings and the occasional Lapland Bunting. Once you

have found them, approach carefully to avoid disturbing them and keep your distance.

Alternatively, turn left at the end of Lady Anne's Drive and carry on along the track until you reach Washington Hide. This overlooks an area of grazing marsh. Further on the track splits into three. Straight on leads to the Joe Jordan Hide which overlooks some pools, while the right-hand track leads to the west end of Holkham pines, an area that regularly holds migrants. The path linking the Washington and Joe Jordan Hides runs along the landward side of the pines, and there is a maze of tracks through the pines to explore. In autumn the pines sometimes harbour thousands of migrating passerines. A long list of rarities has been recorded here, including Britain's only record of Red-breasted Nuthatch. Vagrants from the east are regular and have included Radde's, Dusky, Pallas's, Arctic and Greenish Warblers.

# 2.06 Holkham Hall

An area of parkland, woodland and grassland with an artificial lake.

## Birds

Year round: Tawny Owl, Egyptian Goose, Stock Dove, all three woodpeckers, Treecreeper, Nuthatch
Winter: Black-necked Grebe (regular in recent winters), Goldeneye, Hawfinch was formerly regular in winter and bred in small numbers

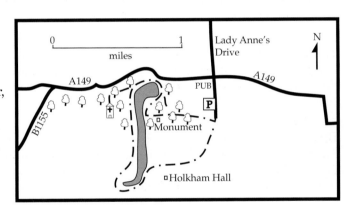

## Location (Car park TF892435)

Signposted south off the A149 coast road between Burnham Overy Staithe and Wells by the Victoria pub. Drive 0.2 miles and turn into the small car park to the right of the entrance road. Walk through the gates and turn right to reach the monument and the lake beyond.

## Management

The parkland is owned and managed by the Holkham Estate.

## Opening times and access

A small pedestrian gate to the left of the main entrance gate is open at all times. There is a car park, tea room and gift shop/art gallery associated with the Hall.

## Other amenities

The Victoria pub by the turning off the main road serves food and provides accommodation. The nearest phone is just east of the Holkham turning on the A149. Other amenities are available in nearby Wells.

## Birdwatching tips

Although resident, the three woodpecker species, particularly Lesser Spotted Woodpecker, are best searched for in early spring when they can be located by call or by their drumming. The area around the monument is one of the better places to listen for Lesser Spotteds.

In winter, Tawny Owls regularly roost on a high perch in the tall cedar tree near the monument and the lake attracts wildfowl, including Egyptian Geese and Goldeneyes, and in recent years a Black-necked Grebe has wintered.

# 2.07 Wells Woods

The eastern end of the extensive Holkham pinewoods is renowned for regularly attracting scarce migrant and vagrant passerines.

## Birds

Spring and autumn: passage migrants, including regular Yellow-browed and Pallas's Warblers in autumn

## Location (Car park TF913455)

Leave the A149 and enter Wells on the B1105. Turn north off this road at the "Pinewoods and Beach" sign and follow the road to the pay and display car park at the end. From the west end of the car park, go through the small gate heading west along the footpath with Wells Boating Lake on your left. At the small information board reached after about 100 yards, the track forks. The sunken area between the trails here is known as the "Dell" and is reknowned for attracting migrants.

## Management

The car park is operated by Pinewoods Caravan Park; the woods are managed by English Nature.

## Opening times and access

There is public access to the woods at all times, although the car park shuts at 10 pm. Parking costs £2 in summer and 50p in winter (end of October to mid-March).

## Other amenities

There is a toilet block, beach cafe, phone and gift shop all in the car park.

## Birdwatching tips

The area known as the Dell is frequently wet underfoot so wellingtons are recommended. This is often the most productive area to search for migrants. Yellow-browed and Pallas's Warblers are annual. The tree and bush cover here is very dense, even in late autumn, so be prepared to spend a considerable time searching for birds.

# 2.08 Warham Greens

A section of the north Norfolk coast, sandwiched between Wells Woods (Site 2.07) and Stiffkey (Sites 2.09 and 2.10), which occasionally holds rarities. The coastal path overlooks a large area of saltmarsh.

## Birds

Spring and autumn: migrant passerines and rarities

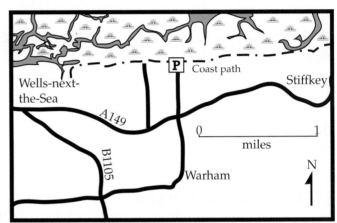

## Location (Car park TF949438)

Take the rough dirt road north from the A149 between Stiffkey and Wells at TF949429 to the small car park at TF949438. If you have the time, it is better to walk along the Peddars Way & Norfolk Coast path from either Wells or Stiffkey, birding the coastal scrub as you go.

## Opening times and access

There is open access along public rights of way. Please keep to the footpaths and do not venture onto the saltmarsh – this can be dangerous and you will disturb breeding and wintering birds.

## Other amenities

These are all available in nearby Wells.

## Birdwatching tips

This area is worth a visit at migration times. Search the hedges, scrubby areas, field margins and sunken pools that edge the coastal footpath.

# 2.09 Stiffkey Woods

A small sycamore wood that attracts migrants, especially in autumn.

## Birds

Autumn: migrant passerines, including regular Yellow-browed Warblers

## Location (Car park TF965439)

Turn north off the A149 at the western end of Stiffkey onto the rough track (Green Way) signposted to the camping and caravan site. Park in the car park at the end and walk east through the trees to search for migrants.

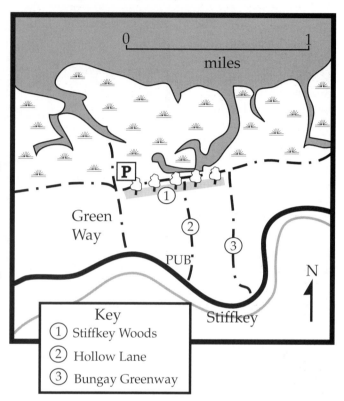

**Key**
1 Stiffkey Woods
2 Hollow Lane
3 Bungay Greenway

## Management

The car park is run by the National Trust.

## Opening times and access

There is public access to the area, but no overnight stays are allowed in the car park.

## Other amenities

There is a phone, shop and pub in Stiffkey and a camping and caravaning site off Green Way, just before the National Trust car park.

## Birdwatching tips

This wood is best visited during periods of easterly winds in the autumn when migrant passerines can be expected. This site regularly attracts Pied Flycatchers, Redstarts and occasionally scarcer migrants, such as Yellow-browed Warblers.

# 2.10 Stiffkey Fen

A small, private marsh, owned by Lord Buxton.

## Birds

Year round: Barn Owl
Spring: Garganey,
Mediterranean Gull
Summer: Avocet,
Lapwing, Redshank,
Oystercatcher, Marsh
Harrier, Reed and Sedge
Warblers
Autumn: passage waders
Winter: Brent and Pink-
footed Geese, Wigeon,
Hen Harrier

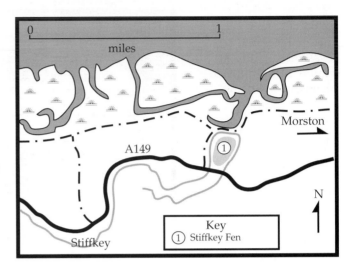

## Location (Car park TF988438)

In Morston, turn north off the A149 to Morston Quay. Park in the National Trust
car park (cost £2) and walk about 1 mile west to view the fen from the seawall.

## Opening times and access

The area is viewable at all times from public footpaths.

## Other amenities

The Red Lion in Stiffkey serves food, there are public toilets at Morston Quay car
park, the nearest garages are in Wells and Blakeney and there is a phone in
Stiffkey.

## Birdwatching tips

Stiffkey Fen can only be viewed from public rights of way; the best vantage point is
from the top of the seawall.

# 2.11 Blakeney Point and Harbour

A windswept shingle point, whose geographical location ensures that it receives good numbers of migrants, especially during the autumn. More than 260 bird species have been recorded.

## Birds

Spring and autumn: migrants, including warblers, pipits, wagtails, chats and thrushes
Summer: Sandwich, Common, Little and Arctic Terns

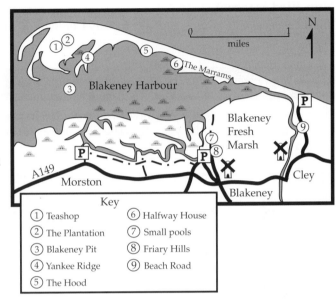

**Key**

1. Teashop
2. The Plantation
3. Blakeney Pit
4. Yankee Ridge
5. The Hood
6. Halfway House
7. Small pools
8. Friary Hills
9. Beach Road

## Location (Information centre TF997460)

This tip of the large shingle spit of Blakeney Point is either a calf-aching three and a half mile walk from Cley Beach car park (TG048458), or a short boat ride from Morston or Blakeney. If walking, it is best to do so at low tide, when you can walk on the exposed firm sand. Boat trips to Blakeney are well-advertised in both Morston and Blakeney villages. Blakeney Harbour itself is worth a diversion off the A149. Walk north from the harbour car park, then east along the Peddars Way & Norfolk Coast path, overlooking some fine areas of saltmarsh.

## Management

National Trust reserve.

## Opening times and access

The area is open at all times, although some areas may be fenced off during the breeding season to prevent disturbance to nesting birds. There is one hide at the point and an information centre and shop is open during peak holiday periods.

## Other amenities

These are all available in Blakeney or Cley. At Cley Beach car park, Arkwrights Cafe is open in the summer and there are public toilets.

## Birdwatching tips

Migration periods, especially autumn, are the best times to visit Blakeney Point. Try to visit during a spell of easterly winds, when the sueda bushes between Halfway House and the point frequently hold large numbers of migrants. These are mainly the commoner species of warblers, chats and flycatchers, but there are always a few scarce migrants, including Bluethroats, Wrynecks and Barred Warblers. A few vagrants are expected annually. During the breeding season, avoid roped off nesting areas and keep away from seals, which may have young with them.

### Non-bird interest
There is a seal colony on the point, mainly Common Seals, although a few Grey Seals are present also.

## 2.12 Cley Marshes

More than 325 species of birds have been recorded at Cley and the reserve is worth visiting at any time of the year. It is the best place on the North Norfolk coast to catch a glimpse of a Bittern.

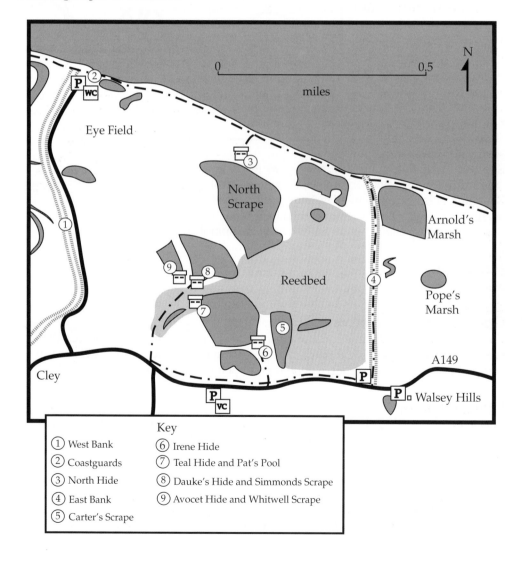

Key

1. West Bank
2. Coastguards
3. North Hide
4. East Bank
5. Carter's Scrape
6. Irene Hide
7. Teal Hide and Pat's Pool
8. Dauke's Hide and Simmonds Scrape
9. Avocet Hide and Whitwell Scrape

## Birds

Year round: Barn Owl, Bearded Tit
Spring and summer: Garganey, Avocet, Whimbrel, Bittern, Marsh Harrier
Autumn: passage waders
Winter: Brent Geese (including regular Black Brants), Hen Harrier, Merlin, Shorelark, Twite, Snow Bunting

## Location (Car park TG054441)

The reserve is situated between the villages of Cley and Salthouse on the A149. The visitor centre is set back on a hill from the A149 and overlooks the marshes. There is one car park here, another at the base of the East Bank and a third at the end of Beach Road where a fee of £1 is payable by non-Norfolk Wildlife Trust members. The Coastliner bus stops on request at the entrance to the visitor centre.

## Management

Managed by the Norfolk Wildlife Trust.

## Opening times and access

The reserve is open all year, but closed Mondays (except bank holiday Mondays). The visitor centre (tel. 01263 740008) is open from 10 am to 5 pm April to October, where you can buy permits. At other times of the year permits may be bought at the warden's house, directions to which are pinned to the visitor centre door. Entry to NWT members is free; for non-members there is an entry fee of £3. There are toilets in the visitor centre and by Arkwrights Cafe at the end of Beach Road. Drinks and sweets are available at the visitor centre, and a wider range of hot and cold food can be bought at Arkwrights Cafe, although this is closed in the winter. There is a boardwalk suitable for wheelchairs from the visitor centre to three hides overlooking the lagoons.

## Other amenities

The nearest garage is in Blakeney, and there are shops, bars and restaurants in Cley. The nearest phone is in Salthouse alongside the main road.

## Birdwatching tips

This reserve is excellent at any time of year. There is a "What's about" board at the visitor centre and it is worth checking the log books in Arkwrights Cafe and Dauke's Hide. June is one of the best months to see Bitterns, when adult birds fly from hunting areas to their nest sites.

## Non-bird interest

Otters occur but are rarely seen.

## The future

The shingle bank protecting Cley and Salthouse Marshes from the North Sea has been breached several times in recent years. This seawall will be replaced with a new sea defence, destroying some of the reserve but affording better protection of what is left. As part of this project, compensatory habitats will be created.

# 2.13 Walsey Hills

A small reserve and migration watchpoint, overlooking Cley marshes.

## Birds
Spring and summer: warblers, passage migrants

## Location (Car park TG060441)
Situated on the south side of the A149, between Cley and Salthouse, signposted as "NOA watchpoint" (marked on Cley map, site 2.12). Park in the small layby at the base of Walsey Hills, adjacent to Snipes Marsh, and follow the footpath up the hillside to the reception hut where you can get a permit.

## Management
NOA reserve.

## Opening times and access
Open at all times. Visitors must report to reception to obtain a permit. The reception hut sells cards and books, with a discount for NOA members. There is a recent sightings board and it is always worth asking for useful birdwatching advice in the area.

## Other amenities
Food and shops are available in Cley, there is a garage in Blakeney and the nearest phone is in Salthouse.

## Birdwatching tips
Walsey Hills is best in spring and autumn for migrants, although it holds a good selection of breeding warbler species.

# 2.14 Salthouse Beach Road

Another area of coastal habitat that regularly holds interesting migrants.

## Birds

Spring: Yellow Wagtail,
Garganey, passage waders
Autumn: passage waders,
Richard's Pipit
Winter: Shorelark, Snow
and Lapland Buntings

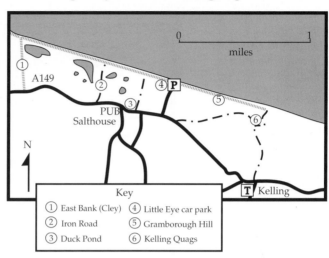

Key
①  East Bank (Cley)  ④ Little Eye car park
②  Iron Road       ⑤ Gramborough Hill
③  Duck Pond       ⑥ Kelling Quags

## Location (Layby overlooking Salthouse pools TG080439, beach car park TG082443)

At the east end of
Salthouse, turn left into Beach Road. Almost immediately pull into a layby and
scan the pools to the west and the meadow on the opposite side of the road.
Continue to the end of Beach Road and park in the Little Eye (Gramborough Hill)
National Trust car park. Salthouse Duck Pond, alongside the A149 just to the west
of the Beach Road turning, is also worth a quick look.

## Opening times and acess

There is open public access at all times.

## Other amenities

There is a pub, shop and phone in Salthouse. The nearest garage is in Blakeney.

## Birdwatching tips

In winter, look for flocks of passerines on the shingle sea bank and the area of low-
lying vegetation and pools behind. Gramborough Hill makes a useful viewpoint for
locating the flocks. Scan the sea for divers. In late autumn, Richard's Pipits are
occasionally found in the grassy fields around here. Mediterranean Gulls are
occasionally present with the groups of Black-headed Gulls around Salthouse that
are accustomed to coming to bread.

# 2.15 Salthouse Heath

A good place for night birding in Norfolk.

## Birds
Spring and summer:
Nightjar, Woodcock,
Woodlark, Tree Pipit,
Nightingale

## Location (TG071425)
In Salthouse, turn south
by the Dun Cow pub,
along Purdy Street. The
road climbs to a
crossroads after 0.8
miles. A further 0.2 miles
beyond is a second
crossroads. Find
somewhere to park and
explore.

## Management
This is an area of
common land.

## Opening times and access
At this busy site, please
view and listen from the
road so as to prevent
disturbance to nesting
birds.

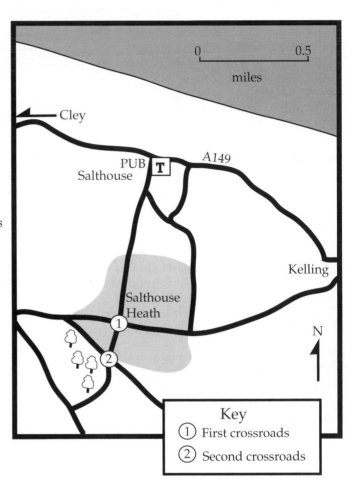

## Other amenties
There is a shop, pub and phone in Salthouse, and a garage in Blakeney.

## Birdwatching tips
Aim to arrive about an hour before dusk to listen for Nightingales and to look for
roding Woodcocks. After sunset, listen and watch over the heath for churring
Nightjars. Note that Nightjars can be heard churring until late July.

# 2.16 Kellings Quags

A NOA reserve east of Salthouse.

## Birds
Spring: early migrants, Garganey
Summer: Black-headed Gull, Avocet

## Location (Car park TG095438)
At the east end of Salthouse, on the A149, turn left signposted "Beach Road" and park at the Little Eye (Gramborough Hill) National Trust car park at the end of the road (see map for site 2.14). Alternatively, just past Baron Art in Kelling there is limited parking on the left at the start of a narrow lane that is unsuitable for motor vehicles. Walk down the lane to view the pool on your right-hand side.

## Management
This area is a NOA reserve.

## Opening times and access
The area is viewable at all times from public rights of way.

## Other amenities
There is a pub in Salthouse, a garage in Blakeney and a phone just south of Baron Art on the Kelling to Holt road. Baron Art has an excellent tea room.

## Birdwatching tips
From the car park at the end of Beach Road, follow the circular walk, first heading east along the sea wall (see map) and look for migrants, e.g. Wheatear, Ring Ouzel and Garganey.

# 2.17 Swanton Novers

A raptor watch-point operated by English Nature, this is the best place in Norfolk to look for Honey Buzzards.

## Birds

Spring and summer: Honey Buzzard (late May to the end of August), Hobby, Common Buzzard, Sparrowhawk, Kestrel

## Location (Car park TG010302)

Situated about seven miles south-west of Holt, the viewpoint is signposted off the north side of the Fulmodeston to Hindolveston road, 0.4 miles west of the junction with the B1110. (Do not follow signs for the village of Swanton Novers). Parking is free.

## Management

The woods belong to Astley Estates and are managed by English Nature, who also operate the Raptor Watch-Point car park.

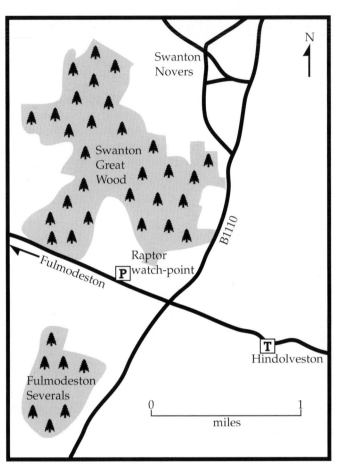

## Opening times and access

The viewpoint is open from mid-May until the end of August, and the car park has an information panel and free information leaflets available.

## Other amenities

There is a phone and a small shop in Fulmodeston.

## Birdwatching tips

English Nature staff or volunteers are usually on site. They warden the Honey Buzzards and can update you on the latest sightings. These rare birds have nested in the surrounding woods since 1989. Note that there is a small population of Common Buzzards in the area, which at distance can be confused with Honey Buzzards.

# Chapter 3: East Norfolk and the Broads

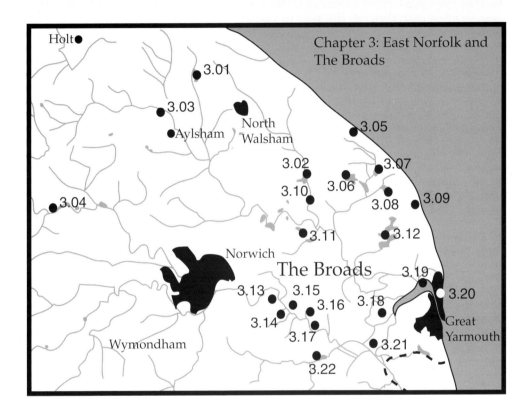

## Introduction

Once, extensive peatlands were found in the lower valleys and tributaries of the rivers Waveney, Yare and Bure. These were excavated for fuel in medieval times, and the rising sea level flooded the peat diggings, creating the network of shallow lakes called the Norfolk Broads. They are famous as a destination for boating holidays, but are rich in wildlife too, including Swallowtail butterflies, Norfolk Hawker dragonflies, Otters and Kingfishers. The alluvial soils further downstream have traditionally been managed as wet grazing marshes, and are home to nesting waders and wintering wildfowl. Geographically, east Norfolk is ideally situated to receive migrant birds, and during spring and autumn regular searching of coastal bushes often pays dividends.

## Special birds

Perhaps the star bird found in the Norfolk Broads is the Common Crane, a small group of which is resident. The other species for which this area is famous is Cetti's

Warbler, which is found in the wet carr woodland surrounding many of the broads and easily located by its explosive "pieces of eight, pieces of eight" song. Along the rivers, Kingfishers can often be seen and the reedbeds are home to Bearded Tits, Marsh Harriers, a small population of Bitterns, and Hen Harriers and Merlins in winter. Buckenham and Cantley Marshes RSPB nature reserves host one of only two regular wintering flocks of Bean Geese in the UK, whilst each year the RSPB wardens the UK's largest colony of Little Terns, at North Denes, Great Yarmouth. Ospreys often pass through the area in spring and autumn and sometimes linger for several weeks.

## Timing

Winter is the time to watch flocks of waterfowl on the grazing marshes and to visit Horsey to see the gathering of roosting Marsh and Hen Harriers, Merlins and perhaps Short-eared Owls. A walk through the flower meadows at Strumpshaw Fen in June is a wonderful experience, especially if you see a Swallowtail butterfly or Norfolk Hawker dragonfly. Late summer and autumn sees good numbers of migrant waders at Cantley Sugar Factory and Breydon Water. In September and October, Yarmouth Cemetery is the place to search for vagrant Yellow-browed and Pallas's Warblers and other exciting migrants.

# 3.01 Gunton Lakes

A classic estate ornamental lake with plenty of old standing dead trees in the surrounding parkland.

## Birds

Year round: woodland birds
Summer: breeding Oystercatcher and Shelduck
Winter: wildfowl

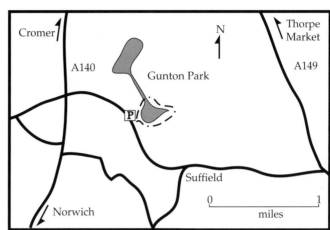

## Location (Car park TG224338)

Located about 6 miles south of Cromer, turn south-east off the A140 Cromer to Aylsham road, 1.8 miles south of Roughton, onto the minor road signposted to Suffield. After 3.8 miles, shortly after passing the impressive gatehouse, turn left into Sawmill Gate car park.

## Management

A private estate.

## Opening times and access

Car parking is free and there is open access along permissive paths only to the southern section of the lake (Saw Mill Pond). On occasions this lake path may be closed on Sundays.

## Other amenities

The nearest petrol station is at Roughton. There is a public phone beyond the turn to Suffield.

## Birdwatching tips

This site is best visited in the winter for wildfowl, which used regularly to include Goosanders. Woodland species can be found in the trees around the car park. Some unusual species have been seen here in the past, including Red-necked Grebe and Marsh Sandpiper.

# 3.02 Barton Broad

There has been a major habitat restoration programme at Barton Broad since 1995. The whole area is part of a National Nature Reserve.

## Birds
Year round: wildfowl

## Location (Car park TG357225)

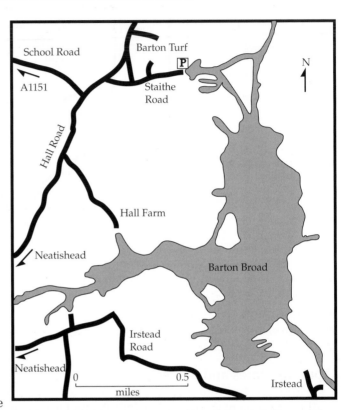

Barton Broad is about 10 miles north-east of Norwich. To reach the north side, turn south-east off the A1151 Norwich to Stalham road at Cat's Common, 4 miles beyond Hoveton, into Smallburgh Road. After three-quarters of a mile, turn left into Mill Road, bear right at the junction reached after 250 yards into School Road and at the T-junction with Hall Road, turn left and bear right into Staithe Road and follow it to the car park. The south end of the Broad is accessed from the minor road between Neatishead and Irstead. Turn off the A1151 into Norwich Road, one mile north-east of Hoveton. At the T-junction reached after a mile, turn left into Street Hill then take the first right, Irstead Road, and follow towards Irstead, with the Broad to your left.

## Management
Norfolk Wildlife Trust reserve.

## Opening times and access
The Broads Authority has built a boardwalk at Heron's Carr at the south end of the Broad, with a viewpoint. Visitors can hire boats during the summer and can take a trip on a purpose-built solar-powered boat (tel. 01692 670779 for details). For more information on access, contact the Broads Authority on 01603 610734 .

## Other amenities
All readily available in Wroxham or Stalham, both on the A1151. There is a public phone in Barton and a pub at Neatishead.

## Birdwatching tips
This site is likely to increase in importance for wildfowl as the habitat improves, following the extensive restoration work carried out.

# 3.03 Blickling Lake

An ornamental lake next to Blickling Hall. It is good for woodland species and wildfowl.

## Birds
Year round: Egyptian Goose, Barn Owl, Lesser Spotted Woodpecker, woodland birds
Winter: wildfowl

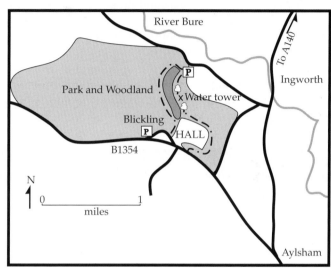

## Location (TG178295)
Situated about 2 miles north of Aylsham, the lake is best accessed from the dam end car park (TG180296). Turn off the A140 Norwich to Cromer road signposted to Ingworth, go through the village and turn right after 1.8 miles, just after crossing the River Bure. Turn right again after 100 yards (signposted to Blickling Lake) and follow this road until you see the car park entrance on the left after about half a mile. Alternatively, you can park by the Buckinghamshire Arms pub (TG176286) in Blickling and walk to the lake from there.

## Management
Managed by the National Trust, primarily as a coarse fishery.

## Opening times and access
There is open access around most of the lake, although it is not possible to walk right around the lake shore, as the grounds of the Hall are located at the southern end of the lake. Car parking is free.

## Other amenities
The Buckinghamshire Arms pub in Blickling sells food. There is a phone by the church in the village. The nearest garage is in Aylsham and petrol is available at the Alby Service Station on the A140 (TG209328).

## Birdwatching tips

Search the lake for wildfowl, passage waders and Common Terns. Goosanders are regular in winter but may be rather shy on this narrow lake. Divers and some of the rarer grebes have occasionally turned up. Barn Owls breed in the park and can often be seen hunting over the grazing meadows on late summer evenings. The east side of the lake is fringed by trees and is good for woodpeckers and other woodland birds. The area just past the water tower is good for Lesser Spotted Woodpecker (best looked for in early spring before the leaves are on the trees). Beech woodland on the surrounding estate occasionally holds singing Wood Warblers in spring. The Weavers Way long-distance footpath, which can be reached across the road from the dam end car park, passes through riverside meadows along the River Bure.

## Non-bird interest

Brown Long-eared Bats hunt in among the tall oaks along the lake edge on summer evenings.

# 3.04 Sparham Pools

Sparham Pools consist of old gravel pits with remnant heath and woodland around the edge.

## Birds

Spring: occasional Osprey, Egyptian Goose, woodland species, Grey Wagtail

## Location (Car park TG073178)

The site is north-west of the village of Lyng in central Norfolk, about 13 miles north-west of Norwich. Take the A1067 Norwich to Fakenham road. Between Lenwade and Bawdeswell (1.2 miles west of Lenwade) turn south towards Lyng. Follow the road down the hill for three-quarters of a mile. The car park is poorly-signposted on the left, at the bottom of the hill (look out for the public footpath and Norfolk Wildlife Trust signs), shortly before the bridge over the River Wensum.

## Management

The site is managed by the Norfolk Wildlife Trust.

## Opening times and access

There is open access and no permit is needed. Wellington boots are essential after winter rain. Contact NWT headquarters (01603 625540) for more details.

## Other amenities

Pub food is available at the Fox and Hounds in Lyng and there is a phone box next to the post office in the village.

## Birdwatching tips

During the spring, woodland birds (both migrants and residents) are well represented around the pit. Many birds breed on the islands in the gravel pit, including Egyptian Geese, Common Terns and Oystercatchers. Ospreys are occasional passage visitors during the spring. Low water levels in some autumns can create good conditions for migrant waders. The bridge over the River Wensum close to the entrance to Sparham Pools is a good place to look for Spotted Flycatchers and Grey Wagtails.

## Non-bird interest

This is a reasonably good site for dragonflies, and the river supports good numbers of Banded Demoiselles from late June to early August.

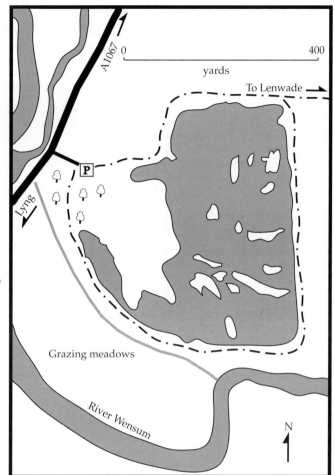

# 3.05 Waxham

A line of sycamores just behind the coastal sea defences makes Waxham a highly attractive spot for passerine migrants, particularly in the autumn.

## Birds

Spring: migrants
Autumn: migrants,
Yellow-browed and
Pallas's Warblers in most
autumns

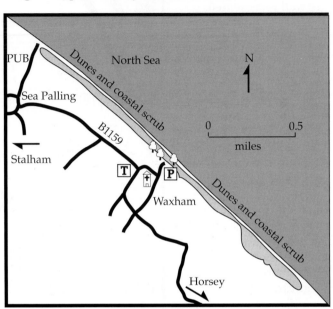

## Location (Car park TG442264)

Waxham is on the coast, just south of Sea Palling on the B1159, about 5 miles east of Stalham. As you enter Waxham going south, the B1159 bends sharp right, but carry on to the left along a minor road, passing the church on your right, then turning left (north) at the T-junction at the end. Park along this track where you can without causing an obstruction and carry on on foot.

## Opening times and access

Open access to the beach and through the woods.

## Other amenities

There is a phone in Waxham, otherwise other amenities are available in Stalham.

## Birdwatching tips

Any piece of scrub can harbour migrants, especially after fall conditions. As you enter the woods, there is a cottage called "Shangri-La" on the right. Check the sycamores and garden of this cottage thoroughly for migrants, but please respect the occupants' privacy. Just before the chalet, a track goes off to the left and underneath the trees. Follow this to the end of the wood, listening carefully for Goldcrest flocks, which sometimes include Firecrests. Carrying on along the main track brings you out of the wood. Walk south along the dunes to find further scrubby vegetation that may hold migrants.

# 3.06 Hickling Broad

An extensive area with a range of Broadland habitats; reedbed, grazing marsh and open water predominate but there is also some mature woodland and carr.

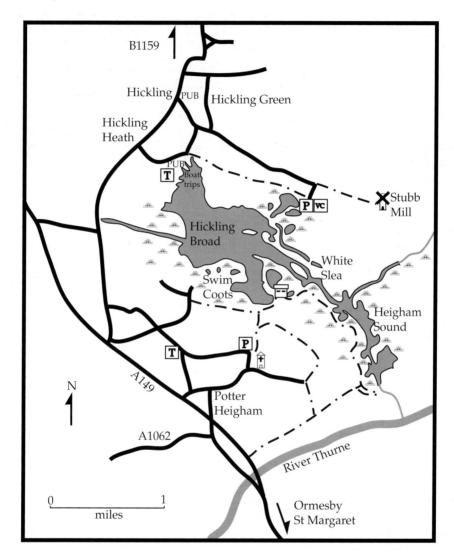

## Birds

Year round: Bittern, Common Crane, Bearded Tit and Marsh Harrier
Spring: Grasshopper and Savi's Warblers, Little Egret, passage waders
Autumn: passage waders
Winter: Hen Harrier, Merlin and Barn Owl

## Location (Car park TG428221 or TG419199)

There are two main access points to Hickling Broad. Hickling village is signposted from the B1159 if coming from the north, or from the A149 near Potter Heigham from the south and west. The NWT Visitor Centre at TG428221 is well signposted from Hickling village. From the road junction by The Greyhound pub, take Stubb Road east for 1.2 miles, then turn right and drive the short distance to the car park.

To access the south side of Hickling, along the Weavers Way long-distance footpath, park at Potter Heigham church at TG419199. Turn left before the church and walk north along the road, with the church to your right. After 200 yards turn right onto a public footpath at a sharp left-hand bend (just after the cemetery). After 50 yards turn left onto the Broads Authority Broads Walk and after 150 yards cross a stile and continue through the wood for another 150 yards to the Weavers Way.

## Management

The site is a National Nature Reserve managed by the Norfolk Wildlife Trust.

## Opening times and access

The visitor centre and reserve is open year-round from 10 am to 5 pm. Adult admission is £2, under 16s and NWT members free. For further details ring 01603 625540. The Weavers Way to the south of the Broad is a public right of way. There are seven hides, overlooking scrapes, meres and reedbed, although some can only be reached by boat. These are by arrangement with the reserve staff who run trips during the summer. This "Water Trail" runs from the Pleasure Boat Inn, May to September. Contact the visitor centre on 01692 598276 for more information.

## Other amenities

The NWT Visitor Centre has toilets and sells snacks and drinks. Food is available at The Greyhound pub in Hickling and the Pleasure Boat Inn at Hickling Heath staithe. Both Hickling and Hickling Green have public phones. There are garages in Stalham and Potter Heigham.

## Birdwatching tips

Bird the scrapes, reedbed and wet grassland from the hides and trails of the reserve. The hide overlooking Rush Hills can be good for passage waders (but is only accessible by boat). Search for Savi's Warbler along Weavers Way or in the vicinity of White Slea.

From the NWT reserve car park walk along Stubb Road to Stubb Mill. In winter this is an excellent viewpoint to look for raptors coming into roost at dusk. Marsh and Hen Harriers, Merlins and Barn Owls are regular. Hickling also regularly hosts the small population of Common Cranes in East Norfolk. These too are often seen going to roost from Stubb Mill in winter.

Hickling Broad has attracted an impressive list of rarities, including Night Heron, Cattle Egret, Glossy Ibis, Marsh Sandpiper and Roller.

## Non-bird interest
Swallowtail butterflies are regular in June. Parts of the reserve grassland are managed using Konik ponies, which originate from Poland.

# 3.07 Horsey Mere

This smaller broad just east of Hickling is a National Trust reserve. Extensive areas of reed, fen and wet grassland fringe the mere.

## Birds
Year round: Bittern, Common Crane, Water Rail, Bearded Tit, Marsh Harrier
Spring: Grasshopper, Savi's and Cetti's Warblers, passage waders
Autumn: passage waders
Winter: Hen Harrier, Merlin, Barn Owl

## Location (Car park TG456223)
The National Trust car park is next to the tourist attraction of Horsey Windpump. This is located along the B1159, about half a mile south of Horsey village, between Sea Palling and West Somerton.

Map labels: Sea Palling, North Sea, Horsey Gap P, Horsey Corner, Brayden Marsh, Horsey Mere, PUB, T, WC, P, V, B1159, West Somerton, N, 0  0.5 miles, V = Viewpoint

## Management
The National Trust acquired the Horsey Estate from the Buxton family in 1948, who still farm and manage the Estate.

## Opening times and access
The Windpump car park costs 30p/hour (free to National Trust members) and closes at 8 pm daily. Horsey Windpump is open April – Sept (11 am to 4.30 pm) and costs £1.30 for adults (free to National Trust members). It can make a good vantage point when searching for raptors. A footpath leads past the Windpump to a viewpoint overlooking the mere and a public footpath runs round the northern side of the mere and along the Waxham Cut, before turning south back to Horsey village. *All other tracks and fields are strictly private – do not park in farm entrances.*

## Other amenities
Toilets (summer only) are located by the National Trust car park.

## Birdwatching tips
Horsey is best visited in September to May. Use the viewpoint to survey for ducks on the mere. Early morning is best, with the sun behind you. On no account wander into the adjacent reedbeds. The path on the northern edge of the mere can be productive for warblers and sometimes Marsh Harriers and Barn Owls, but views are limited by scrub and reed.

Fields either side of the B1159 between Horsey Windpump and West Somerton are probably the best site for finding Common Cranes feeding on old potatoes or winter cereals. These fields also attract Whooper and Bewick's Swans, flocks of Pink-footed and White-fronted Geese, Lapwings and Golden Plovers, and raptors. View from lay-bys along the roadside.

Do not enter areas of scrub or rough grazing marshes at Horsey Gap, where migrant passerines are sometimes found in autumn. Seawatching can be productive during periods of strong onshore winds. Please send any interesting bird sightings to the National Trust Warden, Horsey Windpump, Horsey, Norfolk NR29 4EH.

# 3.08 Martham Broad

A reed-fringed Broad to which there is no access other than by boat, and the site must be viewed from the peripheral public footpaths.

## Birds

Year round: Barn Owl, Kingfisher, Bearded Tit, Cetti's Warbler
Spring and autumn: Marsh Harrier,
Summer: Marsh Harrier, occasional Bittern,
Winter: wildfowl

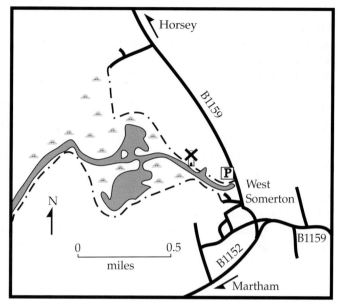

## Location (TG458205)

Martham is located just north of West Somerton on the B1159. Park by the staithe at West Somerton, 0.3 miles from the Lion pub, at (TG469201). The public footpath starting here heads north-west and affords views over the northern section of the Broad. To view the southern section, walk back to the road and into the village, and take the first right (Staithe Road). After the tarmac ends, turn left onto a public footpath which skirts the south side of the Broad. There is no circular route around the site.

## Management

The site is managed by the Norfolk Wildlife Trust.

## Opening times and access

There is open access along the two public footpaths.

## Other amenities

There is a pub in West Somerton. Nearby Horsey Mere has toilets and a snack shop (open during summer). Other facilities are available in nearby Winterton-on-Sea.

## Birdwatching tips

Search the broad and surrounding reedbed for wildfowl and raptors. Barn Owls often hunt over the surrounding grazing marshes on summer evenings.

## Non-bird interest

The Broad and the surrounding network of ditches are good for dragonflies including Norfolk Hawkers.

# 3.09 Winterton Dunes

Coastal dunes, ponds and coastal heath, an increasingly scarce habitat in Norfolk. This site is well worth visiting during spring and autumn migration.

## Birds
Spring and autumn: passage migrants and vagrants
Summer: Little Tern, Nightjar, Stonechat
Winter: Merlin, Hen Harrier

## Location (TG490210)
Winterton is south-east of Waxham and Horsey on the B1159. Turn off the B1159 into the village and follow a dirt track, Beach Road, that leads north-east to the beach car park (TG499197). Tracks lead north and south through the dunes.

## Management
A National Nature Reserve managed by English Nature.

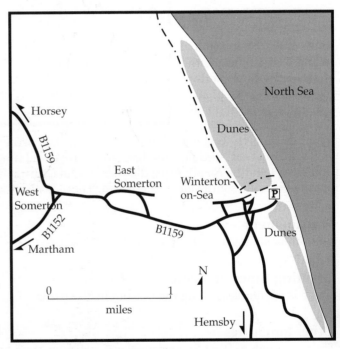

## Opening times and access
Open access at all times.

## Other amenities
These are available in Winterton.

## Birdwatching tips
This is a difficult site to watch, but it is well worth the effort as it regularly turns up good birds. In spring look out for raptors as birds often gather in this area before heading for the Continent, including regular Rough-legged Buzzards. Migrant numbers are seldom high, but search the dunes for chats and wheatears. Rarities recorded here include Red-rumped Swallow, Pied and Isabelline Wheatears and Rose-coloured Starling. Please take great care not to disturb nesting birds on the beach.

## Non-bird interest
Dragonflies are exceptional at this site, and it is one of the few Norfolk sites for Common Hawkers. Pools on the site support populations of the rare Natterjack Toad, and Harbour Porpoises are regular offshore.

# 3.10 How Hill Nature Reserve

Tucked away in the Ant Valley, How Hill Nature Reserve includes a full range of Broadland habitats including some impressive calcareous valley fen communities as well as open water, reedbed, woodland and carr.

## Birds

Year round: Marsh Harrier, Willow Tit
Spring: Osprey, Woodcock, passage waders, Bearded Tit, Wood Warbler, Ring Ouzel
Summer: Hobby, Woodcock, Bearded Tit

## Location (Car park TG372190)

The reserve is well signposted off the A1062 just west of Ludham. Coming from Norwich, turn left down School Lane just before Ludham village (5 miles from Wroxham) and follow signs to the car park (1.2 miles). The parking area is signed "Car park for Toad Hole Cottage and Wildlife Trails".

## Management

Managed as a demonstration nature reserve by the Broads Authority.

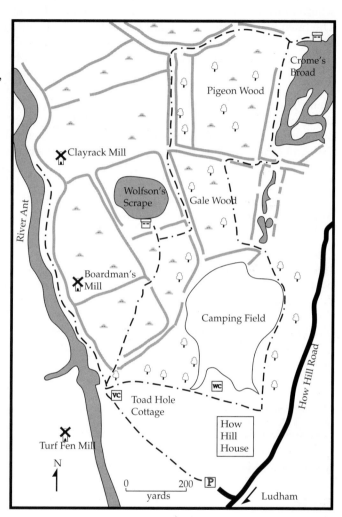

## Opening times and access

Open from 11 am to 5.30 pm from 1 April or Easter (whichever is earlier) to 31 October. During the summer, from 1 June to 30 September, the site is open from 10 am to 6.30 pm. After these times the car park gates may be locked. Permits and trail guides are available from the information centre at Toad Hole Cottage (walk across the lawn from the car park and you will find the centre hidden away on your left). Adult permits cost 50p. Note that trails can be very muddy so wellingtons are recommended.

## Other amenities

The information centre has toilets. Other amenities are available in Ludham.

## Birdwatching tips

The view from the car park overlooks the River Ant and its adjacent marshes where Marsh Harriers are seen year round and Hobbies are regular in summer. The lawn attracts the occasional Ring Ouzel on spring passage. The nature trail starts at Toad Hole Cottage and soon crosses a butterfly meadow on the way to the first hide. This overlooks Wolfson's Scrape, which can hold passage waders when the water levels are suitable. Green and Common Sandpipers and Little Ringed Plovers are regular, while occasional Wood Sandpipers, Greenshanks and Ruffs occur. The nature trail carries on, skirting the edge of Pigeon Wood which was once the temporary home of a Black-and-white Warbler in 1985. It is unlikely anything as exciting as this will occur, but the woods are an excellent place to see Willow Tits and other woodland birds. The second hide overlooks Cromes Broad, where it is possible to see wildfowl and Kingfishers. In May it is a favoured location for passage Ospreys. The trail returns via the Water Gardens to How Hill House. Looking east from either Clayrack or Boardman's Mill at dusk during fine weather in summer is a good way to see roding Woodcocks over the woods.

## Non-bird interest

How Hill is a superb site for invertebrates during the summer. It is perhaps the best site in the Broads to see Swallowtail butterflies, which are on the wing in June. The first meadow on the nature trail is managed specifically for Purple-flowered Meadow Thistle, a preferred nectar source for Swallowtails, and this often allows excellent photographic opportunites of this spectacular insect. The site is also rich in dragonflies, including Norfolk Hawkers (look over ditches with spiky water soldier plants) and Hairy Dragonflies. On still summer evenings you could see Noctule, Daubenton's and Pipistrelle Bats.

# 3.11 Ranworth Broad

A typical Norfolk Broad surrounded by carr woodland. This site attracts passage migrants and is worth watching in the winter for wildfowl.

## Birds

Year round: woodland birds, Marsh Tit, Cetti's Warbler
Spring: Redpoll, Siskin
Winter: large Cormorant roost, wildfowl, Redpoll, Siskin

## Location (Car park TG355154)

Situated about 7 miles north-east of Norwich. Take the B1140 from Norwich, turning left shortly before Panxworth at a junction signposted to Wroxham, Salhouse and Woodbastwick. Immediately after this turning, turn right into a small road signposted to Ranworth. Turn right again at Ranworth church and follow signs to the Conservation Centre car park by the pub. From the car park, backtrack to where the nature trail begins near the staithe (see map).

## Management
Managed by the Norfolk
Wildlife Trust.

## Opening times and access
The NWT Conservation
Centre is open from April
to October between 10 am
and 5 pm. The boardwalk
is free but there is a
charge to visit the Centre.
For more information
phone 01603 625540.

## Other amenities
The nearest toilets are in
the car park opposite The
Maltster's pub in
Ranworth. The Maltster's
serves food. Other
facilities are in nearby
Norwich.

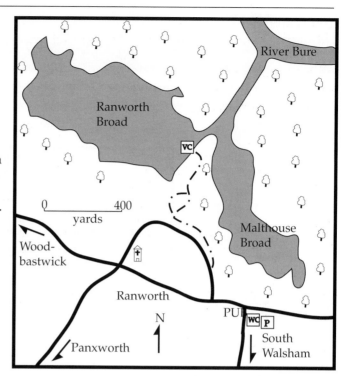

## Birdwatching tips
Check Malthouse Broad and Ranworth Broad for wildfowl. The oak woodland and
carr along the boardwalk is good for woodland birds including Marsh Tits, and
Cetti's Warblers are often heard on the walk to the Conservation Centre. It is
possible to climb Ranworth Church tower which offers a panoramic view of this
area of the Norfolk Broads.

Note: Nearby Wroxham Broad, some 5 miles to the west of Ranworth, tends to get
very disturbed by boats during summer but during winter it is a good site for
wildfowl and a large gull roost.

# 3.12 Flegg Broads (Ormesby, Rollesby and Filby Broads)

This site consists of three interconnected broads. It is difficult to work as access is mainly from road bridges, although one short trail leads to a reed-screen.

## Birds
Winter: occasional Bittern, wildfowl

## Location (TG460148)
Rollesby is on the A149, about 9 miles north-west of Great Yarmouth. Flegg Broad is best viewed from the two road bridges that cross this broads complex. The first of these is along the A149 between Rollesby and Ormesby (TG463153) and the second is on the A1064 between Filby and Burgh St Margaret (TG463136). Both bridges have adjacent car parks.

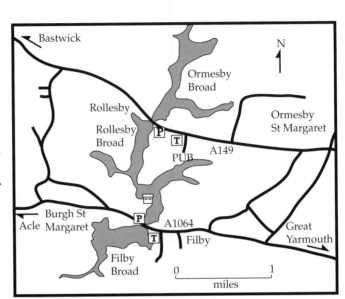

## Opening times and access
View from the bridges and from roadsides overlooking open water areas. Take care when viewing from roads. A trail leads 500 yards from the car park at Filby Bridge to a reed-screen overlooking Little Ormesby Broad.

## Other amenities
There are phones in Rollesby and Filby. The pub at Ormesby serves food.

## Birdwatching tips
This area is best visited in winter when searching through the wildfowl flocks may turn up something interesting. Divers and the rarer grebes appear occasionally.

## Non-bird interest
Look out for Swallowtail butterflies and dragonflies in summer.

# 3.13 Surlingham Church Marsh

A small fen on the River Yare and part of the extensive RSPB Mid Yare Nature Reserve that also includes Strumpshaw Fen (site 3.15), Buckenham and Cantley Marshes (site 3.16) and parts of Rockland Broad (site 3.14).

## Birds

Year round: Cetti's Warbler
Spring and autumn: Marsh Harrier, passage waders

## Location (TG305070)

Surlingham is situated about 5 miles south-east of Norwich. From the A146/A47 junction south-east of Norwich city centre, take the A146 towards Loddon, but turn north after a few hundred yards onto the minor road towards Bramerton. Drive through Bramerton to Surlingham, then turn

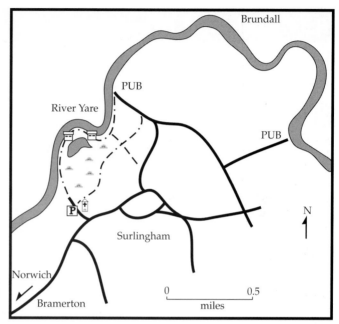

north at TG306065 into Church Lane, signposted to Surlingham Church. Park opposite the church. Against the church wall there is a RSPB sign which includes a map and details of the circular path around the reserve.

## Management
The site is managed by the RSPB.

## Opening times and access
The reserve is accessed along public footpaths and there are two hides. The footpath runs alongside the River Yare and is liable to flooding.

## Other amenities
The Ferry House pub is by the river at TG308076. The nearest phone is in Surlingham.

## Birdwatching tips
This site is undoubtedly underwatched and would repay repeated visits. Rarities in the past have included Savi's Warbler and Green-winged Teal.

## Non-bird interest

Surlingham Church Marsh is a good place to look for Chinese Water Deer. They are especially easy to see when the vegetation has been cut along the reedbed fringes. Ted Ellis, the respected broadland naturalist, is buried in the grounds of the ruined church which overlooks this site.

# 3.14 Rockland Broad

A Broad on the River Yare, part of which belongs to the RSPB's Mid Yare Valley complex of nature reserves (Sites 3.13, 3.15 and 3.16).

## Birds

Year round: Cetti's Warbler
Spring: Marsh Harrier, passage migrants
Summer: Marsh Harrier
Winter: wildfowl, including occasional (Taiga) Bean and White-fronted Geese

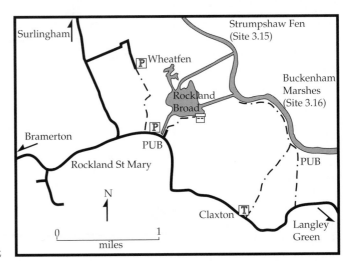

## Location (TG333052)

Situated about 6 miles south-east of Norwich. Take the A146 (Lowestoft road) from Norwich and 0.3 miles after the junction with the A47, turn left at the first set of traffic lights into the minor road to Bramerton and Rockland St Mary. Follow this road for 5.5 miles through Rockland St Mary. Outside the village at the bottom of the hill, just before the New Inn pub and the staithe, is a car park on the left. Park here and cross the wooden bridge. Take the public footpath which runs along the southern bank of the Broad, crosses over two stiles and eventually leads to a hide.

## Management

Part of the site is managed by the RSPB. The shooting rights are owned by Rockland Wildfowlers Association so the site can be disturbed during the shooting season. The Broad itself is owned by Rockland Parish Council.

## Opening times and access

There is open access along the public footpath and one hide.

## Other amenities

The New Inn sells food. The nearest phone is by the post office in Rockland St Mary.

## Birdwatching tips

This site is probably under-watched and does turn up good birds occasionally. Check the alders and willows that fringe the broad for Cetti's Warblers. Check the grazing marshes in winter for geese and raptors. Wildfowl can be seen on the open water visible from the hide. Recent rarities have included a Whiskered Tern.

For a longer walk, carry on past the hide along Short Dyke to the River Yare and follow the river to the Beauchamp Arms pub before turning south towards Claxton and the road that leads back to the staithe.

Another nature reserve – Wheatfen Broad (TG330055) – can be visited on foot from the car park at the staithe. Walk back up the hill towards Rockland St Mary and turn right along the public footpath past Broad Hall Farm. About half a mile along this track is the car park for the reserve. The reserve consists mainly of carr vegetation and supports woodland birds.

## Non-bird interest

The site supports Norfolk Hawker dragonflies during June and July and Brown Argus butterflies can be seen adjacent to the footpath, halfway to the hide, in July and August.

# 3.15 Strumpshaw Fen

Strumpshaw is the centrepiece of the extensive Mid Yare Valley RSPB nature reserves (Sites 3.13, 3.14 and 3.16). Strumpshaw has a variety of wetland habitats typical of the Norfolk Broads. including mature alder carr, fen, fen meadow, willow carr, reedbed, open water and wet grassland.

## Birds

Year round: Marsh Harrier, Kingfisher, Bearded, Marsh and Willow Tits, Cetti's Warbler

Spring and summer: Osprey, Barn Owl, Woodcock, passage waders, Lesser Spotted Woodpecker, Grasshopper Warbler

Autumn: Osprey, Hobby, passage waders

Winter: Hen Harrier, Bittern, Goldeneye, Goosander

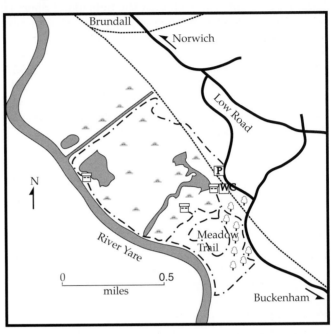

## Location (Car park TG341067)

Turn off the A47 between Norwich and Great Yarmouth, at a well-signposted roundabout, towards Brundall. Drive through Brundall and shortly after leaving the village, turn right into Stone Road and then immediately right again into Low Road (following the brown RSPB sign). Follow this road for about half a mile and park in the reserve car park, just before the railway crossing gates. The reserve is accessed on foot by crossing the railway – take special care when doing so.

## Management

This site is managed by the RSPB. Current management primarily aims to enhance the fen habitats for scarce species and to improve the reedbed for Bitterns.

## Opening times and access

The reserve is open year-round from dawn till dusk, adult entry costs £2.50, free to RSPB members. The area around Staithe Cottage has toilets, bike racks, a visitor information hut (open in the summer only) and a reception hide overlooking the Old Broad. There are a further three hides along the nature trails.

## Other amenities

Available in nearby Brundall.

## Birdwatching tips

The Old Broad Hide, next door to Staithe Cottage, is one of the best places in Norfolk to see Kingfishers. Wintering ducks are also a feature here and occasionally include Smew. During spring and autumn, if the water levels are low, check any muddy margins for passage waders. This is also the first place you are likely to hear the explosive song of the Cetti's Warbler.

The trail beside the cottage passes through woodland before coming to a junction. Turning right takes you along Sandy Wall and past the entrance to the Meadow Trail (open in the summer only). Straight on takes you through some mature alder carr woodland which is good for roding Woodcocks at dusk in the spring and summer. Woodland birds abound here with all three woodpeckers and Siskins and Redpolls in the winter. Golden Orioles are recorded on passage in some springs. This route eventually joins the river, goes left and meets up with the top of Sandy Wall. In some winters Smew and Goosanders have been recorded on the river.

Along the Sandy Wall trail is a turning to the right that leads to Fen Hide. This is a good area for Cetti's Warblers and the hide is a good vantage point for watching Marsh Harriers and Bearded Tits. Check any dead snags for raptors, including Hobbies and Ospreys.

Turn right when you get to the river, to take you to Tower Hide, which overlooks more pools and provides a good viewpoint from which to look for Hen Harriers at dusk in the winter. Bitterns are regular visitors and a small colony of Black-headed Gulls nests here .

Shortly after the Tower Hide the trail heads away from the river and follows the course of the Lackford Run. A viewing area overlooks a small scrape that often hosts migrant waders in spring and autumn, depending on the water levels. From here, continue along the trail to the car park. Willow Tits can be seen in the willow scrub near the railway line.

## Non-bird interest

During the summer the Meadow Trail offers a rare chance to walk in a flower-rich fen-meadow where Swallowtail butterflies and Norfolk Hawker dragonflies can be seen during June. The hawkers favour ditches overgrown with Water Soldier plants. Hairy Dragonflies and Scarce Chasers are possible here too. Red-eyed Damselflies can be seen on the lilies in front of Tower Hide (end of May to early August). Swallowtails can be seen in the garden of the cottage just after you cross the railway line at the end of the Fen Trail. The owners often put a sign up inviting people to enter and enjoy these fantastic butterflies as they drink nectar from garden plants. Chinese Water Deer are often seen in the Mid Yare Valley, usually in reedy places bordering open areas.

# 3.16 Buckenham and Cantley Marshes

This area of pump-drained grassland adjacent to the River Yare is one of the most reliable sites to find the flock of (Taiga) Bean Geese that spend the winter in the Mid Yare Valley (mid-November to early January). This site is close to Strumpshaw Fen (Site 3.15).

## Birds

Spring and summer: waders, Garganey, Grasshopper Warbler
Autumn: passage waders
Winter: Water Pipit, Stonechat, Peregrine, wildfowl, including (Taiga) Bean and White-fronted Geese, Wigeon

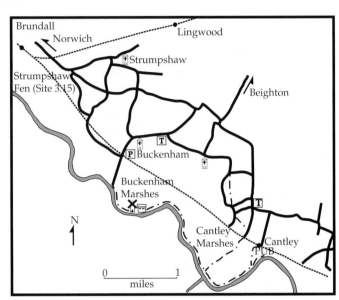

## Location (Car park TG351057 or TG382036)

Buckenham Marshes are reached from Norwich by taking the A47 towards Acle and Great Yarmouth. Turn right towards Brundall at the well-signposted roundabout. Carry on through Brundall and shortly after leaving the village, turn right into Stone Road and carry on, past the sign to the RSPB reserve at Strumpshaw Fen. Turn right, shortly after passing the household waste disposal site on your left, to Buckenham and after the dogleg, turn right into Station Road (signposted to Buckenham railway station). Park by the old station buildings (TG351057) and cross the railway. Follow the dirt road to the river and turn left towards the disused windpump.

Alternatively, continue along the road that passes the entrance to Strumpshaw Fen and turn right at the T-junction. Cross over the manned level crossing and past the cottage, following the road parrallel to the railway, and then follow it round as it turns towards the river. Drive down this bumpy track to the end of the straight where it joins the river bank. Park here and walk towards the derelict tower to the side of which is the hide.

## Management

Buckenham and Cantley came under the management of the RSPB in 1994/5 and the changes in the grazing and flooding regimes have enhanced this site for wintering wildfowl and breeding waders.

## Opening times and access

The site is accessible only along the public footpaths that run around the periphery of the site. There is one hide.

## Other amenities

Brundall has shops and pubs. The nearest petrol station is by the roundabout on the A47. There is a phone near Cantley (see map).

## Birdwatching tips

A telescope is essential. Views of any Bean Geese are likely to be poor, with birds no closer than about three-quarters of a mile away. Any closer approach to the birds makes them fly off, so please take great care not to disturb them in this way. During the winter, the wet fields at Buckenham hold many Wigeons and smaller numbers of other ducks. Look for geese flocks as you walk to the hide. Occasionally the birds can be 'scoped feeding across the river on Claxton Marshes. At this time of the year, Buckenham is one of the most reliable sites in Norfolk for Water Pipits, and each evening there is a spectacular winter dusk flight of up to 20,000 corvids which is best viewed from Buckenham Railway Station. During summer flooded areas are maintained for breeding ducks and waders. Listen out for Grasshopper Warblers in the spring. The site has attracted rarities in the past, including Lesser White-fronted Goose and Marsh Sandpiper.

## Non-bird interest

Norfolk Hawker, Hairy Dragonfly and Scarce Chaser dragonflies have all been seen here in recent years. Search along the ditches either side of the access track from the railway crossing to the river.

# 3.17 Cantley Sugar Factory

This beet sugar factory and its associated silt settling ponds lie next to the River Yare (just downstream from the Mid Yare Valley nature reserves – sites 3.13–3.16) and attracts migrant waders and other waterbirds during spring and autumn.

## Birds

Year round: Cetti's Warbler, Kingfisher
Spring and autumn: Marsh Harrier, Black Redstart, passage waders
Summer: Marsh Harrier, Black Redstart, breeding ducks and waders
Winter: Water Pipit, wildfowl

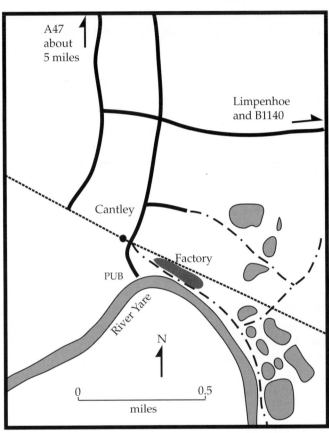

## Location (TG382036)

Cantley is situated about 2 miles west of the B1140 Acle to Beccles road, via the village of Limpenhoe which is signposted from the B1140. Cantley is signposted from the A47, between Brundall and Acle and from Buckenham Marshes (Site 3.16). Park on the roadside by Cantley railway station. Cross the railway and turn left into the British Sugar works. Take extreme care within the factory area where the public footpath route is marked on the road and pavement in yellow. The circular footpath eventually crosses the railway then turn left onto the path which leads to Grange Road in Cantley. It is best to bring an OS map to ensure that you stay on public rights of way.

## Management

The site is a working sugar beet processing factory managed by British Sugar.

## Opening times and access

The public footpaths do not provide good views over the main birding areas – the settling ponds. Areas not served by public footpaths are strictly off-limits. However, British Sugar often arranges special access if a rarity is present. It is safest to visit this site at weekends when vehicular traffic around the site is at a minimum.

## Other amenities

There is a phone in Langley Road (the last turning on the right before the railway line). There is a riverside pub that serves food, and accommodation and garages are available in nearby Acle.

## Birdwatching tips

Black Redstarts occasionally breed around the factory buildings. This site is excellent for passage waders during spring and autumn migration when you should search for them on any viewable silt ponds with exposed mud. Deeper pools sometimes attract Black-necked Grebes. If shooting is taking place on the surrounding marshes, care should be taken not to flush birds and send them over the guns. Past rarities at this site include Spoonbill, Baird's and Marsh Sandpipers, Wilson's Phalarope and Caspian Tern.

# 3.18 Berney Marshes

Berney Marshes is a 360 ha reserve consisting of wet grassland, shallow floods and a small amount of reed that forms part of the immense Halvergate Marshes, a large expanse of grazing marsh of high importance for nature conservation. Part of the reserve overlooks the southern end of Breydon Water (Site 3.19). Berney Marshes is undoubtedly under-watched.

## Birds

Spring: Garganey, passage waders
Summer: Avocet, breeding waders and wildfowl
Autumn: passage migrants
Winter: wildfowl, Short-eared Owl

## Location (TG465050)

Berney Marshes is north of Breydon Water, west of Great Yarmouth. There is no access by car, making this one of the more remote birding spots in Norfolk. You can either walk the 4 miles to the reserve along the northern bank of Breydon Water or take a train from Great Yarmouth that

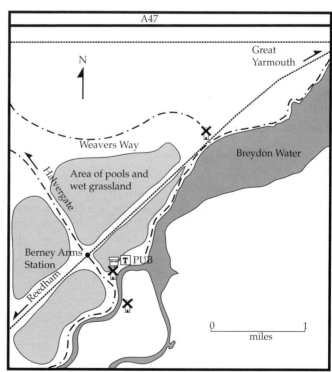

makes a request stop at Berney Arms (cost for a single £1.10). Trains run most frequently on Sundays. Asda supermarket in Great Yarmouth kindly allows birdwatchers to park in their car park when they visit Berney Marshes. It is recommended to take a train to Berney and then walk back along the length of the reserve to Great Yarmouth. A trip to Berney Marshes is an adventure and you will usually have the reserve pretty much to yourself when you get there.

## Management
The nature reserve is managed by the RSPB who have raised the water levels on the wet grassland, making this a bird-rich oasis among the surrounding pump-maintained grazing marsh.

## Opening times and access
There is open access along public footpaths and no permits are needed. There is one birdwatching screen with a bench seat, but no hides.

## Other amenities
A picnic site is close to the windmill (the latter is open in the summer) and a shop selling basic food stuffs is located next door to the Berney Arms pub, which also sells food during the summer. There is also a phone nearby.

## Birdwatching tips
In spring, search for Garganeys on flooded pools and ditches. Passage waders favour the muddy margins of the main pool visible from the birdwatching screen. Temminck's Stints and Spoonbills are regular here. In winter, look out for hunting Barn and Short-eared Owls, Rough-legged Buzzards, Peregrines and Merlins. At this time of year, flocks of Wigeons, Teals, Shovelers, Pink-footed Geese, Lapwings and Golden Plovers are present, sometimes totalling around 40,000 birds. December and January are the best months. It is also worth checking the river and the south end of Breydon Water, as well as the small reedbed by the pub. The buildings at Ashtree Farm sometimes attract Black Redstarts during migration. Geographically the reserve is ideally placed to attract rarities (especially during very high tides on Breydon Water) and these have included American Wigeon, Greater Yellowlegs, Terek Sandpiper, Collared Pratincole and Great Reed Warbler.

## Non-bird interest
Berney and the surrounding wet grassland and associated ditches are good for dragonflies. Follow the Weavers Way long-distance footpath towards Halvergate, where it is possible to see the Variable Damselfly and Norfolk Hawker along the ditches. These two special dragonflies are not present on the reserve, probably because the water is too brackish, but Hairy Dragonfly occurs.

# 3.19 Breydon Water

A large estuary at the confluence of the three major Broadland rivers that attracts numerous passage waders and supports important populations of wintering wildfowl. The site regularly holds rarities.

## Birds
Spring: Caspian Tern and Kentish Plover are both regular, passage waders
Summer: breeding terns
Autumn: passage waders (including rarities)
Winter: waders and wildfowl

## Location (TG490070)
Driving into Great Yarmouth from the west on the A47, continue straight on at the first roundabout. At the second roundabout do a U-turn and the Asda superstore is signposted on the left. Asda has kindly agreed to allow birdwatchers to use their car park (TG519082), located behind Great Yarmouth railway station. From Asda walk along the edge of the estuary towards and then under the bridge. Beyond the bridge you will see a hide further along the path and the broad expanse of the estuary. Another hide overlooks the tern nesting rafts about half a mile further on.

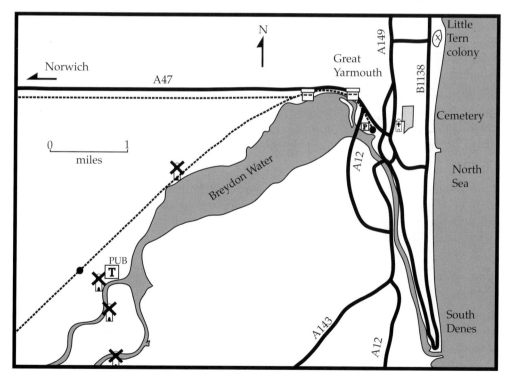

## Management
Breydon Water is managed in partnership by the RSPB, English Nature, Great Yarmouth Naturalists' Society, Great Yarmouth Wildfowlers' Association and the Broads Authority.

## Opening times and access
There is open access along footpaths and to the public hides. Parking in the Asda car park is free.

## Other amenities
Asda sells petrol, a wide range of food and has phones. There are toilets at Asda during opening times.

## Birdwatching tips
At high tide, areas in front of the first hide throng with waders and you may be lucky and find a rarity. The list of rarities recorded at this site is very impressive and includes Greater Sandplover, Greater Yellowlegs, Terek Sandpiper and Ring-billed Gull. Mediterranean Gulls are regularly seen here, but are best looked for along the nearby seafront in Great Yarmouth (Site 3.20).

# 3.20 Great Yarmouth

This east coast harbour town contains several sites that are worth visiting and is next door to Breydon Water (Site 3.19).

## Birds
Year round: Mediterranean Gull
Spring and autumn: passage migrants
Summer: Little Tern
Winter: Purple Sandpiper

## Location (TG530060)
Great Yarmouth is situated on the east coast and reached by taking the A47 from Norwich. The following places within the town are of interest:

The cemeteries at TG528082 can be accessed by driving into Great Yarmouth on the A47 (from Norwich), go straight over at the first two roundabouts, then turn left at the traffic lights into Northgate Street, then right at the first mini-roundabout into Kitchener Road. Park on Kitchener Road where there is a cemetery on both sides of the road and explore. If you have trouble parking here, carry on down Kitchener Road, turn right at the end and there is a large pay and display car park on the left. The site is worth visiting during migration.

The Little Tern colony at TG532099 is on the beach north of the town. It is reached by taking the A149 (signposted to Caister) north out of town. Turn right at the traffic lights onto Jellicoe Road signposted to the Racecourse. Go over the bridge and turn left into North Drive. Park and walk towards the beach.

To get to the harbour entrance at TG533038, head south down Marine Parade (which becomes South Beach Parade), past all the tourist attractions into the South Denes industrial area. There is a car park at the harbour entrance on the left.

## Other amenities
These are all available in Great Yarmouth.

## Birdwatching tips
Mediterranean Gulls are present year-round along the seafront north of the town. Take some bread along. The Little Tern colony (the largest in the UK) is worth a visit during summer. Please view from a distance to avoid disturbing the birds. Do not enter the fenced area.

The two cemeteries can be excellent for passage migrants in spring and autumn. Many rare species have been recorded here, including Red-flanked Bluetail, Siberian Thrush, and Arctic, Hume's and Dusky Warblers.

The harbour entrance can be good for gulls and Purple Sandpipers in winter (check the groynes). Nearby South Denes industrial estate (TG533045) has breeding Black Redstarts in summer.

# 3.21 Chedgrave and Langley Marshes

An isolated and undisturbed area of Broadland grazing marsh that occasionally hosts interesting birds. The area is huge and can only be covered on foot. A telescope is essential.

## Birds
Winter: raptors, wildfowl

## Location (TG450020)
The area about 7 miles south-east of Great Yarmouth is best accessed from the A143 Great Yarmouth to Beccles road, north-east of Haddiscoe. From Haddiscoe, head towards Great Yarmouth, then turn right after 1.5 miles, shortly after crossing the bridge over the railway line and New Cut drainage ditch, into the road that leads to the Spinnaker Restaurant (TM455994). Park here and take the public footpath north-west along New Cut (signposted "No unauthorised vehicular access"). Alternatively, continue along the A143 and turn left into the boatyard, just before the bridge over the River Waveney, by the public footpath sign (TM456995). Park and follow the public footpath signs through the buildings. After the last building take the path along the top of the bank, between the grazing marsh and the reedbed and river.

## Management
Private grazing marsh.

## Opening times and access
Open access along public footpaths.

## Other amenities
Available in nearby Great Yarmouth.

## Birdwatching tips
Chedgrave is best visited during winter, when the site occasionally hosts a Rough-legged Buzzard and the Bean Goose flock from the Yare Valley is sometimes present.

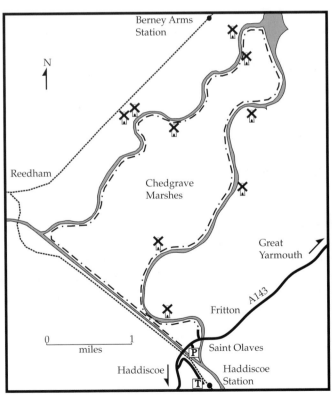

# 3.22 Hardley Flood

A large reed-fringed expanse of water that occasionally turns up interesting birds, especially wildfowl.

## Birds
Year round: wildfowl

## Location (TM382996)
Turn off the A146 Norwich to Lowestoft road, about 7 miles south-east of Norwich, to Chedgrave. From the crossroads in the centre of the village, turn east along Hardley Road. Shortly after passing the church on your right, turn right and follow the road to the boatyards. Park by the

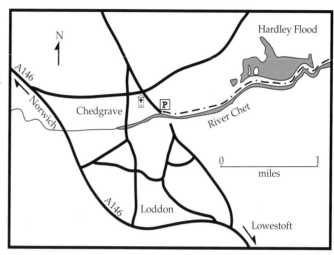

gate and public footpath sign and follow the footpath along the river bank for about a mile, past the reedbed, pools and dead trees to Hardley Flood.

## Management
Privately managed.

## Opening times and access
Open access along public rights of way.

## Other amenities
These are available in nearby Loddon.

## Birdwatching tips
Search the flood for wildfowl and other wetland birds. Some shooting takes place during winter at this site, which may affect the number of birds present. Low water levels in spring and autumn may leave mud exposed and attract waders. Rarities at this site have included Blue-winged Teal and Black-winged Stilt.

# Chapter 4: The Brecks

## Introduction

During the retreat of the last ice age, boulder clay was deposited across the whole of southern Britain. One area, however, was not affected by this process and rather than getting a covering of fertile clay from the retreating glaciers, the 150 square miles roughly centred around Thetford remained uncovered. All that was left was the poor undersoil that supported an impoverished flora. This has led to distinctive habitat changes as you enter the Brecks. Although much of the poor soils were once covered in heathland, a lot of the area has now been planted with coniferous forests, this being the only use to which the area, which was too poor to support extensive agriculture, could be put. Several coniferous woodland and heathland species have their outposts in East Anglia, making a visit to the Brecks a rewarding experience for the birdwatcher.

## Special birds

The Brecks include one of the only sites in the UK where the presence of Goshawks is advertised, and people are encouraged to look for them displaying during late winter/early spring. In addition, a well-managed site allows comfortable viewing of breeding Stone Curlews where access is arranged so that there is no danger of disturbing these sensitive and rare birds. From May onwards, visitors are able to visit the only advertised breeding site in the UK for Golden Orioles. Although egg collecting has been a problem at this site in the past, the RSPB are employing a policy of openness, wardening the site and setting up a temporary car park and viewpoint for visitors wishing to see the birds.

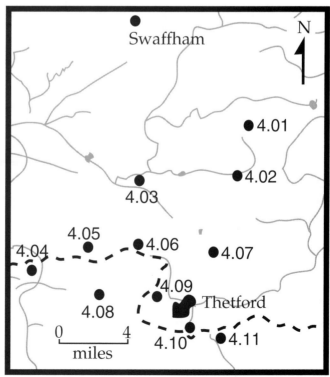

As if the above three species were not enough, the forests in the Brecks also host the following in good numbers: Hobbies, Woodcocks, Golden Pheasants, Tree Pipits, Crossbills, around 12% of the UK's Nightjars and around 25% of the UK's Woodlarks. They are also the sole East Anglia breeding site for Siskins and provide reliable places to look for Hawfinches, especially in winter.

## Timing

A visit on a calm sunny day in late winter/early spring should give a good chance of seeing Woodcocks, Crossbills, Woodlarks and Siskins, and this is easily the best time of the year for finding Goshawk, Golden Pheasants and Hawfinches, while it is just possible that an early Stone Curlew may already have arrived.

A visit any time from mid-May onwards should provide opportunities for seeing Golden Orioles, Hobbys, Woodcocks, Tree Pipits, Woodlarks and Nightjars.

# 4.01 Wayland Wood

An ancient semi-natural woodland that is one of the best places to see the introduced Golden Pheasant in Norfolk.

## Birds

Year round: Golden Pheasant, woodland birds

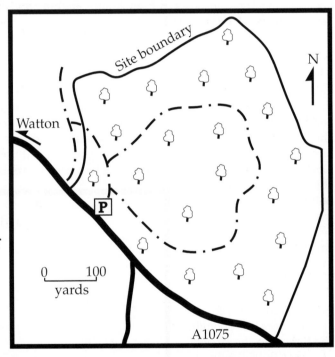

## Location (Car park TL923996)

Take the A1075 Thetford road out of Watton (past Tescos) for about a mile and Wayland Wood is the first piece of woodland on your left. The small car park is on the left about 100 yards past the start of the wood.

## Management

Norfolk Wildlife Trust reserve.

## Opening times and access

The reserve is open at all times and no permit is needed. The trails can be very wet, especially in winter.

## Other amenities

These are available in nearby Watton.

## Birdwatching tips

Search the network of trails for Golden Pheasants which can usually be heard calling, but may be difficult to see.

## Non-bird interest

Wayland has an excellent woodland ground flora (best in spring).

# 4.02 Thompson Water

A shallow artificial lake fringed by reeds.

## Birds

Year round: wildfowl
Spring: Ruddy Duck,
passage waders
Summer: Ruddy Duck

## Location (Car park TL914946)

Turn off the A1075, 2.1 miles south of the B1108/ A1075 intersection in Watton, signposted to Thompson. Carry straight on at the crossroads reached after 1.4 miles. At a sharp right-hand bend in the road go straight ahead onto a broad dirt track. Ignore the first out-of-date Ministry of Defence (MOD) sign by the now permanently open gate. Turn left by the next gate. Park in the signed car park and walk to the lake to view. CARE: this site is on the edge of a MOD firing range.

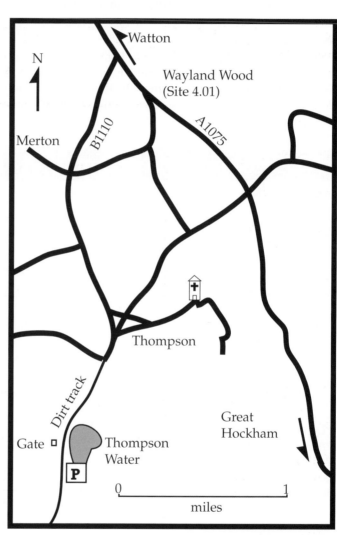

## Management

Norfolk Wildlife Trust reserve.

## Opening times and access

Free parking and access on foot from the car park. The tracks around the lake are rather narrow for wheelchairs, although access to the lake shore from the car park should be straightforward. There are no hides. A trail guide is available from the NWT headquarters on receipt of a SAE. For more information, call 01603 625540.

## Other amenities
Available in nearby Watton.

## Birdwatching tips
Thompson Water is a fairly small, reed-fringed lake which provides one of the few regular sites in Norfolk for the introduced Ruddy Duck. The lake has turned up good birds in the past, notably in spring 1999 when a Pied-billed Grebe took up residence in reeds at the southern end of the lake.

## Non-bird interest
The woodland and heath of nearby Thompson Common to the north and west of the lake has numerous small pools, harbouring several species of dragonfly including Scarce Emerald Damselfly. However, much of the land around here is MOD land, so be careful where you walk and do not ignore red flags when they are flying.

# 4.03 Lynford Arboretum

An attractive arboretum in the heart of the Brecks.

## Birds
Winter and spring: Crossbill, Hawfinch, Lesser Spotted Woodpecker, Siskin, Nuthatch, Redpoll

## Location (Car park TL823943)
Leave Mundford north on the A1065. After 0.4 miles, turn right, signposted "Lynford Hall" and "Arboretum". Follow the road past Lynford Hall and park in the car park on the left-hand side after 1 mile.

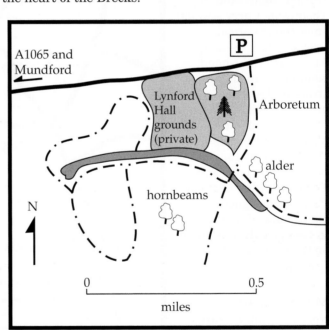

## Management
Part of Thetford Forest Park, and managed by Forest Enterprise.

## Opening times and access
Public access at all times on foot to the lake and surrounding wood, but not to the private Lynford Hall grounds. The wide trails are suitable for disabled visitors and a disabled visitor track runs alongside the stream. Dogs are not allowed. For more information, call Forest Enterprise on 01842 810271.

## Other amenities

None on site, but all are readily available in nearby Mundford.

## Birdwatching tips

Noted as one of the most reliable sites for Hawfinches, and, particularly in early spring on calm sunny mornings, for Lesser Spotted Woodpeckers. The best place to see Hawfinches is the large isolated hornbeam trees, where the birds sometimes feed on the ground beneath, usually in the early morning. They are also sometimes seen in hawthorn hedges along the entrance road. In some years Crossbills can be very numerous in the scattered conifer trees between the car park and the lake. Redpolls and Siskins are most regular in winter. Both species are often found in small flocks in the alder trees bordering the lake and stream that runs from it. Listen carefully for calling Lesser Spotted Woodpeckers, which have nested along the track by the stream. Lynford Arboretum is very popular. Try to avoid visiting at weekends and try to get there early in the morning. The ornamental lake has some wildfowl, but is unlikely to hold much of interest.

# 4.04 Lakenheath

This popular site for viewing Golden Orioles is now part of an RSPB nature reserve where the RSPB is creating a massive reedbed. The reserve will open in about 2004 (currently there is only a temporary carpark) and will add a new dimension to birding in the Brecks.

## Birds

Spring and summer: Golden Oriole, Barn Owl, Hobby, waders, Egyptian Goose

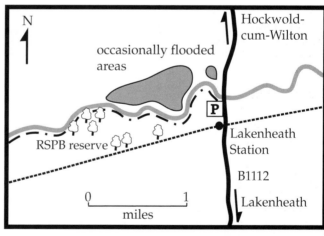

## Location (Car park TL723864)

Turn west off the A1065, signed to Eriswell, 2.1 miles north of the Barton Mills roundabout on the A11. Carry on through Lakenheath and continue north until you cross over the railway line, 6.2 miles from the A1065 turning. About 100 yards after the railway, there is a temporary car park on the left-hand side of the road. Cross the stile and follow the footpath west along the raised bank on the south bank of the river with the large wet fen to your right. After half a mile there is a poplar plantation to the left with a track through it, closed by a locked gate. *On no account go beyond the gate into the plantation*. Watch from the footpath for orioles. About another quarter of a mile further along the raised bank is a second plantation with poplars, another place that the orioles frequent.

## Management
Wardened by the RSPB during the summer.

## Opening times and access
Public access at all times along the footpath from the car park. The footpath would be suitable for disabled visitors, apart from negotiating the stiles along the path. There are no hides, but a viewpoint may be arranged overlooking an orioles' nest once the eggs have hatched successfully.

## Other amenities
None on site, but all are readily available in nearby Lakenheath.

## Birdwatching tips
Orioles are best seen shortly after they arrive in the spring – normally around the second week of May, when there is little leaf cover on the poplars. At this time, the males are active, calling a lot and flying around the wood and they are readily heard on still days from the footpath. The orioles sing at any time of the day, but are much more active early in the morning. A good strategy is to watch along the ride that stretches out beyond the gate. Birds are frequently seen crossing it.

Look for waders and ducks on the wet flash to the north of the river bank. In late spring and summer Hobbies are a frequent sight here, catching dragonflies over the water.

# 4.05 Weeting Heath

A small area of acid grassland, maintained by intensive rabbit grazing. At one time similar habitat, together with heather-dominated vegetation, would have covered large areas of the Brecks.

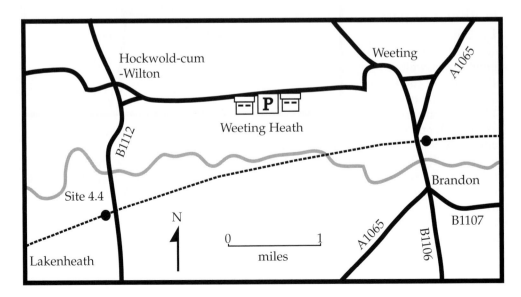

## Birds
Spring and summer: Stone Curlew, Woodlark, Wheatear

## Location (Car park TL758879)
From the traffic lights where the B1067 meets the A1065 in Brandon, drive north on the A1065 for 0.5 miles, then bear left on the minor road signposted to Weeting. After 0.6 miles turn left, signed to Hockwold-cum-Wilton. Weeting Heath is signposted on the left-hand side after a further 0.2 miles.

## Management
Norfolk Wildlife Trust reserve.

## Opening times and access
Access is on foot and permits to enter the reserve cost £2 for adults, but are free for children under 16 and NWT members. The wide trails are suitable for disabled visitors and should allow easy access to the two hides although viewing may be difficult. The reserve is open from dawn until dusk from 1 April until September. For more information, call NWT on 01603 625540.

## Other amenities
All readily available in nearby Brandon.

## Birdwatching tips
A visit early or late in the day (within the opening times) is highly recommended as the Stone Curlews are more likely to be active. Although there are several sites in the Brecks where Stone Curlews can be seen from public roads and rights of way, it is strongly recommended that you visit Weeting Heath. The views here are likely to be much better than any you can obtain elsewhere and you do not run the risk of disturbing these rare birds.

# 4.06 Santon Downham

A circular trail through a variety of Breckland forest habitats. This site was one of the last breeding haunts of the Red-backed Shrike in England.

## Birds

Year round: Lesser Spotted Woodpecker, Nuthatch, Treecreeper, Siskin, Redpoll
Spring and summer: Woodcock, Nightjar, Woodlark, Hawfinch
Winter: occasional Great Grey Shrike

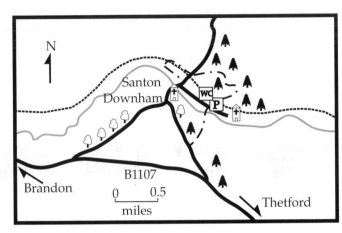

## Location (Car park TL828873)

From the B1107 Brandon to Thetford road, take the minor loop road signposted to Santon Downham. One end is on the outskirts of Brandon, 0.8 miles from the A1065, B1107 junction. The other is 2.8 miles from the A11 Thetford bypass. On reaching the village of Santon Downham, take the minor road north-east, signposted to Santon Warren, by the church. Pass the Forest Commission District Office on your left (from where a guide leaflet to the area can be obtained: office opening hours 9 am to 4 pm on weekdays) and after 0.3 miles turn right along a minor track between the Little Ouse River and the railway line, signposted to St Helens. After 0.6 miles you reach St Helens car park on your left. There are toilets (including a disabled toilet), swings and barbecues around the car park (call 01842 810271 in advance if you are planning to use the latter).

## Management

Forest Enterprise.

## Opening times and access

Public access on foot at all times. The wide trails are suitable for disabled visitors. Parking at Santon Downham is free, but the St Helens car park costs £1, April to October. Call Forest Enterprise on 01842 810271 for more details.

## Other amenities

These are all readily available in either Thetford or Brandon.

## Birdwatching tips

The 3.5 mile Bird Trail marked by orange-topped posts is recommended. It follows a circular loop from the car park and passes through a mixture of broad-leaved and coniferous woodland and open areas. Check cleared areas for Woodlarks, which are most readily found by hearing them singing, mainly in the early morning and particularly on calm, still days in early spring (late February to early March).

They can often be seen near the car park. These open areas are also good for Nightjars and roding Woodcocks on summer evenings. Golden Pheasants occur at Santon Downham but are not easy to see. Hawfinches are occasionally seen in the tops of the tall trees that line the minor road between Brandon and Santon Downham and in the village itself. It is also worth a quick look in Santon Downham churchyard as Firecrests occasionally turn up here.

### Non-bird interest
This site is good for Banded Demoiselle damselflies along the Little Ouse during June and July. Daubenton's Bats hunt along the river at dusk on summer evenings. The heathland along the north side of the railway has a good variety of Breckland flora.

## 4.07 East Wretham

A heath in the heart of the Brecks with some pleasant birdwatching, especially during winter when flocks of finches and other small birds are often present.

### Birds
Year round: Tawny Owl
Spring and summer: waders, Nightjar, Redstart, Tree Pipit
Autumn: waders
Winter: ducks, Siskin, Crossbill

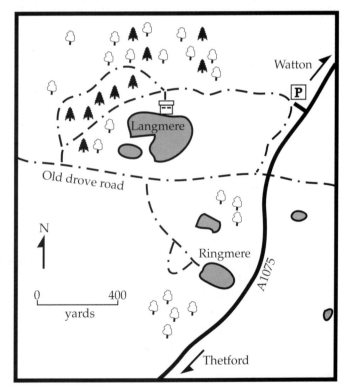

### Location (Car park TL911881)
Situated on the A1075 between Watton and Thetford, the reserve car park is well signposted to the west of this road, about half a mile south-east of the village of East Wretham.

### Management
Norfolk Wildlife Trust reserve.

### Opening times and access
The reserve is open daily throughout the year, from 8 am until dusk. Entry and car parking is free and access is on foot only. There is one hide, overlooking Langmere.

## Other amenities
These are all available in nearby Watton to the north or Thetford to the south.

## Birdwatching tips
The open heathland walk from the warden's house towards Langmere is a good place to see common birds like Goldcrests and Skylarks. The hawthorn scrub regularly holds singing Tree Pipits and the mixed woodland Redstarts, both in the spring and summer. In winter, open areas attract flocks of finches and buntings.

The hide overlooking Langmere is always worth a look. This, and the nearby Ringmere, are natural lakes fed by rising ground water. Their water levels vary throughout the year, and they may even dry up completely. However, when there are areas of exposed mud around the edges during spring and autumn, passage waders are often present. At other times, ducks are seen in small numbers.

# 4.08 Mayday Farm

Mayday Farm is a good place to access the extensive Thetford Forest.

## Birds
Year round: Crossbill, Siskin
Spring and summer: Goshawk, Curlew, Nightjar, Woodcock, Woodlark, Tree Pipit
Winter: Goshawk, Woodcock, Woodlark

## Location (Car park TL790830)
Turn north-west off the A11 in the village of Elveden, situated between Thetford and Mildenhall, onto the B1106, signposted to Brandon. After 2.8 miles, turn left just after a house along a rough track signposted (the signpost is on the

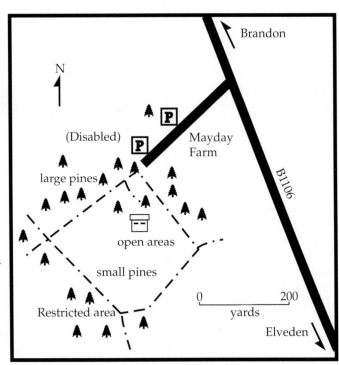

north side of the B1106) to "Mayday Bird Hide". Park after 150 yards in the car park on the right-hand side, or if a disabled visitor, carry on a further 350 yards to the disabled car park. Explore the forest trails on foot. Note: don't leave valuables in your car; this area is notorious for break-ins.

## Managment
Forest Enterprise.

## Opening times and access
Free car parking and open access to the walking trails at all times. The wide trails are suitable for disabled visitors although the furthest parts of the main circular track may prove a little rough for wheelchairs. Large areas are marked as "No public access" during much of the breeding season and at times of forestry felling. There is one birdwatching hide. Call Forest Enterprise on 01842 810271 for more information.

## Other amenities
None on site, but all are readily available in nearby Thetford, Brandon or Mildenhall.

## Birdwatching tips
Probably the main attraction is Goshawk but to see this species you will need a great deal of patience or plenty of luck! The best strategy is to visit Mayday Farm on a still, bright, sunny day in late February or early March. These are the ideal conditions for Goshawks to be displaying. Be prepared for a lengthy wait in the bird hide or stand at the edge of a large clearing where you have a good view over the forest and wait.

# 4.09 Thetford Warren

Another good access point to Thetford Forest. There is a possibility of finding Goshawk and it is a good place to search for Woodlarks.

## Birds
Spring and summer: Goshawk, Nightjar, Woodcock, Woodlark, Tree Pipit, Crossbill, Siskin

## Location (Car park TL842841)
From the roundabout on the A11 Thetford bypass, take the B1107 to Brandon. After 1 mile, shortly after passing the Thetford Golf Club sign, pull off on the left-hand side into a rough sandy car park at the Thetford Warren and Rishbeth Wood and Forest Walk sign. Walk south-west about 300 yards, passing the ruined Thetford Warren Lodge on your right to the Thetford Forest Park Rishbeth Wood sign. Any clearfell areas in the forest are suitable habitat for Woodlark and Nightjar. In 2001, two good clearings could be reached by turning sharp left at the Thetford Forest Park Rishbeth Wood sign and following the line of posts with red tops. After 400 yards, you entered a large clearing. Carrying straight across this brought you back into forest, where, after passing a small clearing on the right, there was a second large clearing. The situation with clearings will change over the years, and you should either seek out clearings yourself or contact the High Lodge Visitor Centre for latest information, or, during office hours, contact the Forest Enterprise District Offices at Santon Downham (Site 4.06 for details).

## Management

Part of Thetford Forest
Park, managed by Forest
Enterprise.

## Opening times and access

Open public access on foot
with wide trails suitable
for disabled visitors. Car
parking is free. There is a
Forest Drive from the
High Lodge which costs,
depending on the season,
£2–£3. Call Forest
Enterprise on 01842
810271 for more
information.

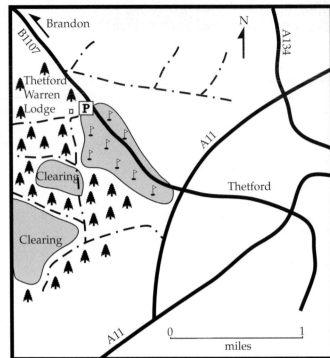

## Other amenities

All readily available in
nearby Thetford. Food is
available in the High Lodge visitor centre.

## Birdwatching tips

Woodlarks are usually quite easy to find, particularly on calm spring days in any
clearfell areas. These clearings are good places to see Goshawks – again calm early
spring mornings are best. Crossbills and Siskins are sometimes numerous in
conifer trees around the edge of the clearings. From mid-April, Tree Pipits are
common in the clearings and at dusk Nightjars may readily be found hawking over
the clearings when Woodcocks can be seen roding. Forest rides on the east side of
the B1107 as marked on the map can be productive for Woodcocks, Nightjars and
Siskins.

# 4.10 Barnhamcross Common

An area of common land on the outskirts of Thetford. The area is popular with dog walkers so a visit in the early morning is recommended when there is less chance of disturbance.

## Birds
Year round: Hawfinch

## Location (Car park TL866817)
From the A11/A134 roundabout to the west of Thetford, drive south-east on the A134 for 1.6 miles, passing a school on your right. Pull off the A134 onto a rough car park on the left just beyond the last houses.

## Opening times and access
Common land with public access on foot and free parking.

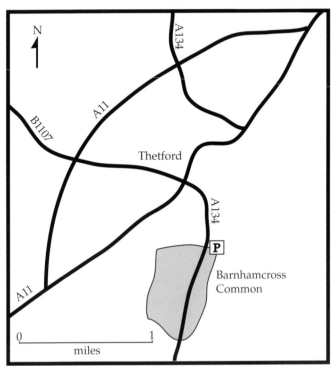

## Other amenities
All are readily available in Thetford.

## Birdwatching tips
From the car park, explore the open common and heathland particularly to the east and north of the road. Hawfinches are regularly seen in the area, especially around the pumping station about 300 yards north-east of the car park. They have been recorded at all times of the year, although winter is the most reliable season.

## Norfolk species list

All species on the British Ornithologists' Union (BOU) British List in categories A to C that have occurred in Norfolk up to the end of November 2000 are shown below. Also included are the two widely recognised yellow-legged gull forms, Caspian Gull *Larus cachinnans* and Yellow-legged Gull *L. michahellis*, and two others not identified to species, an albatross sp., *Thalassarche* sp. and Fea's/Zino's Petrel *Pterodroma feae/madeira*. Family names follow Clements (2000) *Birds of the World: A Checklist*.

### Gaviidae (Divers)
..... Red-throated Diver *Galvia stellata*
..... Black-throated Diver *Gavia arctica*
..... Great Northern Diver *Gavia immer*
..... White-billed Diver *Gavia adamsii*

### Podicipedidae (Grebes)
..... Pied-billed Grebe *Podilymbus podiceps*
..... Little Grebe *Tachybaptus ruficollis*
..... Great Crested Grebe *Podiceps cristatus*
..... Red-necked Grebe *Podiceps grisegena*
..... Slavonian Grebe *Podiceps auritus*
..... Black-necked Grebe *Podiceps nigricollis*

### Diomedeidae (Albatrosses)
..... Albatross sp. *Thalassarche* sp.

### Procellariidae (Shearwaters and Petrels)
..... Fulmar *Fulmarus glacialis*
..... Fea's/Zino's Petrel *Pterodroma feae/madeira*
..... Black-capped Petrel *Pterodroma hasitata*
..... Cory's Shearwater *Calonectris diomedea*
..... Great Shearwater *Puffinus gravis*
..... Sooty Shearwater *Puffinus griseus*
..... Manx Shearwater *Puffinus puffinus*
..... Mediterranean Shearwater *Puffinus yelkouan*
..... Little Shearwater *Puffinus assimilis*

### Hydrobatidae (Storm-petrels)
..... Storm Petrel *Hydrobates pelagicus*
..... Leach's Petrel *Oceanodroma leucorhoa*

### Sulidae (Boobies and Gannets)
..... Gannet *Morus bassanus*

### Phalacrocoracidae (Cormorants)
..... Cormorant *Phalacrocorax carbo*
..... Shag *Phalacrocorax aristotelis*

### Ardeidae (Herons, Egrets, Bitterns)
..... Bittern *Botaurus stellaris*
..... Little Bittern *Ixobrychus minutus*
..... Night Heron *Nycticorax nycticorax*
..... Squacco Heron *Ardeola ralloides*
..... Cattle Egret *Bubulcus ibis*
..... Little Egret *Egretta garzetta*

..... Great White Egret *Egretta alba*
..... Grey Heron *Ardea cinerea*
..... Purple Heron *Ardea purpurea*

### Ciconiidae (Storks)
..... Black Stork *Ciconia nigra*
..... White Stork *Ciconia ciconia*

### Threskiornithidae (Ibises and Spoonbills)
..... Glossy Ibis *Plegadis falcinellus*
..... Spoonbill *Platalea leucorodia*

### Anatidae (Ducks, Geese and Swans)
..... Mute Swan *Cygnus olor*
..... Bewick's Swan *Cygnus columbianus*
..... Whooper Swan *Cygnus cygnus*
..... Bean Goose *Anser fabalis*
..... Pink-footed Goose *Anser brachyrhynchus*
..... White-fronted Goose *Anser albifrons*
..... Lesser White-fronted Goose *Anser erythropus*
..... Greylag Goose *Anser anser*
..... Snow Goose *Anser caerulescens*
..... Canada Goose *Branta canadensis*
..... Barnacle Goose *Branta leucopsis*
..... Brent Goose *Branta bernicla*
..... Red-breasted Goose *Branta ruficollis*
..... Egyptian Goose *Alopochen aegyptiacus*
..... Ruddy Shelduck *Tadorna ferruginea*
..... Shelduck *Tadorna tadorna*
..... Mandarin Duck *Aix galericulata*
..... Wigeon *Anas penelope*
..... American Wigeon *Anas americana*
..... Gadwall *Anas strepera*
..... Teal *Anas crecca*
..... Green-winged Teal *Anas carolinensis*
..... Mallard *Anas platyrhynchos*
..... Pintail *Anas acuta*
..... Garganey *Anas querquedula*
..... Blue-winged Teal *Anas discors*
..... Shoveler *Anas clypeata*
..... Red-crested Pochard *Netta rufina*
..... Pochard *Aythya ferina*
..... Canvasback *Aythya valisineria*
..... Ring-necked Duck *Aythya collaris*
..... Ferruginous Duck *Aythya nyroca*
..... Tufted Duck *Aythya fuligula*
..... Scaup *Aythya marila*
..... Eider *Somateria mollissima*

..... King Eider *Somateria spectabilis*
..... Steller's Eider *Polysticta stelleri*
..... Long-tailed Duck *Clangula hyemalis*
..... Common Scoter *Melanitta nigra*
..... Surf Scoter *Melanitta perspicillata*
..... Velvet Scoter *Melanitta fusca*
..... Bufflehead *Bucephala albeola*
..... Goldeneye *Bucephala clangula*
..... Smew *Mergus albellus*
..... Red-breasted Merganser *Mergus serrator*
..... Goosander *Mergus merganser*
..... Ruddy Duck *Oxyura jamaicensis*

### Accipitridae (Hawks, Eagles and Kites)
..... Honey Buzzard *Pernis apivorus*
..... Black Kite *Milvus migrans*
..... Red Kite *Milvus milvus*
..... White-tailed Eagle *Haliaeetus albicilla*
..... Marsh Harrier *Circus aeruginosus*
..... Hen Harrier *Circus cyaneus*
..... Montagu's Harrier *Circus pygargus*
..... Goshawk *Accipiter gentilis*
..... Sparrowhawk *Accipiter nisus*
..... Common Buzzard *Buteo buteo*
..... Rough-legged Buzzard *Buteo lagopus*
..... Golden Eagle *Aquila chrysaetos*

### Pandionidae (Osprey)
..... Osprey *Pandion haliaetus*

### Falconidae (Falcons and Caracaras)
..... Kestrel *Falco tinnunculus*
..... Red-footed Falcon *Falco vespertinus*
..... Merlin *Falco columbarius*
..... Hobby *Falco subbuteo*
..... Gyr Falcon *Falco rusticolis*
..... Peregrine *Falco peregrinus*

### Phasianidae (Pheasants and Partridges)
..... Red-legged Partridge *Alectoris rufa*
..... Grey Partridge *Perdix perdix*
..... Quail *Coturnix coturnix*
..... Pheasant *Phasianus colchicus*
..... Golden Pheasant *Chrysolophus pictus*

### Rallidae (Rails, Gallinules and Coots)
..... Water Rail *Rallus aquaticus*
..... Spotted Crake *Porzana porzana*
..... Little Crake *Porzana parva*
..... Baillon's Crake *Porzana pusilla*
..... Corncrake *Crex crex*
..... Moorhen *Gallinula chloropus*
..... Allen's Gallinule *Porphyrula alleni*
..... Coot *Fulica atra*

### Gruidae (Cranes)
..... Common Crane *Grus grus*

### Otididae (Bustards)
..... Little Bustard *Tetrax tetrax*
..... Great Bustard *Otis tarda*

### Haematopodidae (Oystercatchers)
..... Oystercatcher *Haematopus ostralegus*

### Recurvirostridae (Avocets and Stilts)
..... Black-winged Stilt *Himantopus himantopus*
..... Avocet *Recurvirostra avosetta*

### Burhinidae (Thick-knees)
..... Stone Curlew *Burhinus oedicnemus*

### Glareolidae (Pratincoles and Coursers)
..... Cream-coloured Courser *Cursorius cursor*
..... Collared Pratincole *Glareola pratincola*
..... Oriental Pratincole *Glareola maldivarum*
..... Black-winged Pratincole *Glareola nordmanni*

### Charadriidae (Plovers and Lapwings)
..... Little Ringed Plover *Charadrius dubius*
..... Ringed Plover *Charadrius hiaticula*
..... Kentish Plover *Charadrius alexandrinus*
..... Greater Sand Plover *Charadrius leschenaultii*
..... Caspian Plover *Charadrius asiaticus*
..... Dotterel *Charadrius morinellus*
..... American Golden Plover *Pluvialis dominica*
..... Pacific Golden Plover *Pluvialis fulva*
..... Golden Plover *Pluvialis apricaria*
..... Grey Plover *Pluvialis squatarola*
..... Sociable Plover *Chettusia gregaria*
..... Lapwing *Vanellus vanellus*

### Scolopacidae (Sandpipers and Allies)
..... Knot *Calidris canutus*
..... Sanderling *Calidris alba*
..... Semipalmated Sandpiper *Calidris pusilla*
..... Red-necked Stint *Calidris ruficollis*
..... Little Stint *Calidris minuta*
..... Temminck's Stint *Calidris temminckii*
..... White-rumped Sandpiper *Calidris fuscicollis*
..... Baird's Sandpiper *Calidris bairdii*
..... Pectoral Sandpiper *Calidris melanotos*
..... Sharp-tailed Sandpiper *Calidris acuminata*
..... Curlew Sandpiper *Calidris ferruginea*
..... Purple Sandpiper *Calidris maritima*
..... Dunlin *Calidris alpina*
..... Broad-billed Sandpiper *Limicola falcinellus*
..... Stilt Sandpiper *Micropalama himantopus*
..... Buff-breasted Sandpiper *Tryngites subruficollis*
..... Ruff *Philomachus pugnax*
..... Jack Snipe *Lymnocryptes minimus*
..... Common Snipe *Gallinago gallinago*
..... Great Snipe *Gallinago media*
..... Long-billed Dowitcher *Limnodromus scolopaceus*
..... Woodcock *Scolopax rusticola*
..... Black-tailed Godwit *Limosa limosa*
..... Bar-tailed Godwit *Limosa lapponica*

..... Little Whimbrel *Numenius minutus*
..... Whimbrel *Numenius phaeopus*
..... Curlew *Numenius arquata*
..... Spotted Redshank *Tringa erythropus*
..... Redshank *Tringa totanus*
..... Marsh Sandpiper *Tringa stagnatilis*
..... Greenshank *Tringa nebularia*
..... Greater Yellowlegs *Tringa melanoleuca*
..... Lesser Yellowlegs *Tringa flavipes*
..... Solitary Sandpiper *Tringa solitaria*
..... Green Sandpiper *Tringa ochropus*
..... Wood Sandpiper *Tringa glareola*
..... Terek Sandpiper *Xenus cinereus*
..... Common Sandpiper *Actitis hypoleucos*
..... Spotted Sandpiper *Actitis macularia*
..... Turnstone *Arenaria interpres*
..... Wilson's Phalarope *Phalaropus tricolor*
..... Red-necked Phalarope *Phalaropus lobatus*
..... Grey Phalarope *Phalaropus fulicarius*

## Stercoraiidae (Skuas and Jaegers)
..... Pomarine Skua *Stercorarius pomarinus*
..... Arctic Skua *Stercorarius parasiticus*
..... Long-tailed Skua *Stercorarius longicaudus*
..... Great Skua *Stercorarius skua*

## Laridae (Gulls)
..... Mediterranean Gull *Larus melanocephalus*
..... Laughing Gull *Larus atricilla*
..... Franklin's Gull *Larus pipixcan*
..... Little Gull *Larus minutus*
..... Sabine's Gull *Larus sabini*
..... Bonaparte's Gull *Larus philadelphia*
..... Black-headed Gull *Larus ridibundus*
..... Slender-billed Gull *Larus genei*
..... Ring-billed Gull *Larus delawarensis*
..... Common Gull *Larus canus*
..... Lesser Black-backed Gull *Larus fuscus*
..... Herring Gull *Larus argentatus*
..... Yellow-legged Gull *Larus michahellis*
..... Caspian Gull *Larus cachinnans*
..... Iceland Gull *Larus glaucoides*
..... Glaucous Gull *Larus hyperboreus*
..... Great Black-backed Gull *Larus marinus*
..... Ross's Gull *Rhodosstethia rosea*
..... Kittiwake *Rissa tridactyla*
..... Ivory Gull *Pagophila eburnea*

## Sternidae (Terns)
..... Gull-billed Tern *Gelochelidon nilotica*
..... Caspian Tern *Sterna caspia*
..... Lesser Crested Tern *Sterna bengalensis*
..... Sandwich Tern *Sterna sandvicensis*
..... Roseate Tern *Sterna dougallii*
..... Common Tern *Sterna hirundo*
..... Arctic Tern *Sterna paradisaea*
..... Sooty Tern *Sterna fuscata*
..... Little Tern *Sterna albifrons*
..... Whiskered Tern *Chlidonias hybridus*
..... Black Tern *Chlidonias niger*
..... White-winged Black Tern *Chlidonias leucopterus*

## Alcidae (Auks, Murres and Puffins)
..... Guillemot *Uria aalge*
..... Razorbill *Alca torda*
..... Black Guillemot *Cepphus grylle*
..... Little Auk *Alle alle*
..... Puffin *Fratercula arctica*

## Pteroclidae (Sandgrouse)
..... Pallas's Sandgrouse *Syrrhaptes paradoxus*

## Columbidae (Pigeons and Doves)
..... Rock Dove *Columba livia*
..... Stock Dove *Columba oenas*
..... Woodpigeon *Columba palumbus*
..... Collared Dove *Streptopelia decaocto*
..... Turtle Dove *Streptopelia turtur*
..... Rufous Turtle Dove *Streptopelia orientalis*

## Psittacidae (Parrots, Macaws and Allies)
..... Ring-necked Parakeet *Psittacula krameri*

## Cuculidae (Cuckoos)
..... Great-spotted Cuckoo *Clamator glandarius*
..... Cuckoo *Cuculus canorus*

## Tytonidae (Barn-owls)
..... Barn Owl *Tyto alba*

## Typical Owls (Strigidae)
..... Scops Owl *Otus scops*
..... Snowy Owl *Nyctea scandiaca*
..... Little Owl *Athene noctua*
..... Tawny Owl *Strix aluco*
..... Long-eared Owl *Asio otus*
..... Short-eared Owl *Asio flammeus*
..... Tengmalm's Owl *Aegolius funereus*

## Caprimulgidae (Nightjars and Allies)
..... Nightjar *Caprimulgus europaeus*

## Apodidae (Swifts)
..... Swift *Apus apus*
..... Pallid Swift *Apus pallidus*
..... Pacific Swift *Apus pacificus*
..... Apline Swift *Apus melba*

## Alcedinidae (Kingfishers)
..... Kingfisher *Alcedo atthis*

## Meropidae (Bee-eaters)
..... Bee-eater *Merops apiaster*

## Coraciidae (Typical Rollers)
..... Roller *Coracias garrulus*

## Upupidae (Hoopoe)
..... Hoopoe *Upupa epops*

## Picidae (Woodpeckers and Allies)
..... Wryneck *Jynx torquilla*
..... Green Woodpecker *Picus viridis*
..... Great Spotted Woodpecker *Dendrocopos major*
..... Lesser Spotted Woodpecker *Dendrocopos minor*

## Alaudidae (Larks)
..... Calandra Lark *Melanocorypha calandra*
..... White-winged Lark *Melanocorypha leucoptera*
..... Short-toed Lark *Calandrella brachydactyla*
..... Woodlark *Lullula arborea*
..... Skylark *Alauda arvensis*
..... Shore Lark *Eremophila alpestris*

## Hirundinidae (Swallows)
..... Sand Martin *Riparia riparia*
..... Swallow *Hirundo rustica*
..... Red-rumped Swallow *Hirundo daurica*
..... House Martin *Delichon urbica*

## Motacillidae (Wagtails and Pipits)
..... Richard's Pipit *Anthus novaeseelandiae*
..... Blyth's Pipit *Anthus godlewskii*
..... Tawny Pipit *Anthus campestris*
..... Olive-backed Pipit *Anthus hodgsoni*
..... Tree Pipit *Anthus trivialis*
..... Meadow Pipit *Anthus pratensis*
..... Red-throated Pipit *Anthus cervinus*
..... Rock Pipit *Anthus petrosus*
..... Water Pipit *Anthus spinoletta*
..... Yellow Wagtail *Motacilla flava*
..... Citrine Wagtail *Motacilla citreola*
..... Grey Wagtail *Motacilla cinerea*
..... Pied Wagtail *Motacilla alba*

## Bombycillidae (Waxwings)
..... Waxwing *Bombycilla garrulus*

## Dulidae (Dippers)
..... Dipper *Cinclus cinclus*

## Troglodytidae (Wrens)
..... Wren *Troglodytes troglodytes*

## Prunellidae (Accentors)
..... Dunnock *Prunella modularis*
..... Alpine Accentor *Prunella collaris*

## Muscicapidae (Old World Flycatchers)
..... Robin *Erithacus rubecula*
..... Thrush Nightingale *Luscinia luscinia*
..... Nightingale *Luscinia megarhynchos*
..... Bluethroat *Luscinia svecica*
..... Red-flanked Bluetail *Tarsiger cyanurus*
..... Black Redstart *Phoenicurus ochruros*

..... Redstart *Phoenicurus phoenicurus*
..... Whinchat *Saxicola rubetra*
..... Stonechat *Saxicola torquata*
..... Isabelline Wheatear *Oenanthe isabellina*
..... Wheatear *Oenanthe oenanthe*
..... Pied Wheatear *Oenanthe pleschanka*
..... Black-eared Wheatear *Oenanthe hispanica*
..... Desert Wheatear *Oenanthe deserti*
..... Spotted Flycatcher *Muscicapa striata*
..... Red-breasted Flycatcher *Ficedula parva*
..... Collared Flycatcher *Ficedula albicollis*
..... Pied Flycatcher *Ficedula hypoleuca*

## Turdidae (Thrushes and Allies)
..... Rock Thrush *Monticola saxatilis*
..... White's Thrush *Zoothera dauma*
..... Siberian Thrush *Zoothera sibirica*
..... Ring Ouzel *Turdus torquata*
..... Blackbird *Turdus merula*
..... Black-throated Thrush *Turdus ruficollis*
..... Fieldfare *Turdus pilaris*
..... Song Thrush *Turdus philomelos*
..... Redwing *Turdus iliacus*
..... Mistle Thrush *Turdus viscivorus*

## Cisticolidae (Cisticolas and Allies)
..... Fan-tailed Warbler *Cisticola juncidis*

## Sylviidae (Old World Warblers)
..... Cetti's Warbler *Cettia cetti*
..... Pallas's Grasshopper Warbler *Locustella certhiola*
..... Lanceolated Warbler *Locustella lanceolata*
..... Grasshopper Warbler *Locustella naevia*
..... River Warbler *Locustella fluviatilis*
..... Savi's Warbler *Locustella luscinioides*
..... Aquatic Warbler *Acrocephalus paludicola*
..... Sedge Warbler *Acrocephalus schoenobaenus*
..... Paddyfield Warbler *Acrocephalus agricola*
..... Blyth's Reed Warbler *Acrocephalus dumetorum*
..... Marsh Warbler *Acrocephalus palustris*
..... Reed Warbler *Acrocephalus scirpaceus*
..... Great Reed Warbler *Acrocephalus arundinaceus*
..... Booted Warbler *Hippolais caligata*
..... Icterine Warbler *Hippolais icterina*
..... Melodious Warbler *Hippolais polyglotta*
..... Dartford Warbler *Sylvia undata*
..... Subalpine Warbler *Sylvia cantillans*
..... Sardinian Warbler *Sylvia melanocephala*
..... Ruppell's Warbler *Sylvia rueppelli*
..... Desert Warbler *Sylvia nana*
..... Barred Warbler *Sylvia nisoria*
..... Lesser Whitethroat *Sylvia curruca*
..... Whitethroat *Sylvia communis*
..... Garden Warbler *Sylvia borin*
..... Blackcap *Sylvia atricapilla*
..... Greenish Warbler *Phylloscopus trochiloides*
..... Arctic Warbler *Phylloscopus borealis*
..... Pallas's Warbler *Phylloscopus proregulus*
..... Yellow-browed Warbler *Phylloscopus inornatus*
..... Hume's Warbler *Phylloscopus humei*
..... Radde's Warbler *Phylloscopus schwarzi*

..... Dusky Warbler *Phylloscopus fuscatus*
..... Western Bonelli's Warbler *Phylloscopus bonelli*
..... Wood Warbler *Phylloscopus sibilatrix*
..... Chiffchaff *Phylloscopus collybita*
..... Willow Warbler *Phylloscopus trochilus*

## Regulidae (Kinglets)
..... Goldcrest *Regulus regulus*
..... Firecrest *Regulus ignicapillus*

## Paradoxornithidae (Parrotbills)
..... Bearded Tit *Panurus biarmicus*

## Aegithalidae (Long-tailed Tits)
..... Long-tailed Tit *Aegithalos caudatus*

## Paridae (Chickadees and Tits)
..... Marsh Tit *Parus palustris*
..... Willow Tit *Parus montanus*
..... Coal Tit *Parus ater*
..... Blue Tit *Parus caeruleus*
..... Great Tit *Parus major*

## Sittidae (Nuthatches)
..... Red-breasted Nuthatch *Sitta canadensis*
..... Nuthatch *Sitta europaea*

## Tichodromidae (Wallcreeper)
..... Wallcreeper *Tichodroma muraria*

## Certhiidae (Creepers)
..... Treecreeper *Certhia familiaris*

## Remizidae (Penduline Tits)
..... Penduline Tit *Remiz pendulinus*

## Oriolidae (Old World Orioles)
..... Golden Oriole *Oriolus oriolus*

## Laniidae (Shrikes)
..... Isabelline Shrike *Lanius isabellinus*
..... Red-backed Shrike *Lanius collurio*
..... Lesser Grey Shrike *Lanius minor*
..... Great Grey Shrike *Lanius excubitor*
..... Woodchat Shrike *Lanius senator*

## Corvidae (Crows, Jays and Magpies)
..... Jay *Garrulus glandarius*
..... Magpie *Pica pica*
..... Nutcracker *Nucifraga caryocatactes*
..... Jackdaw *Corvus monedula*
..... Rook *Corvus frugilegus*
..... Carrion Crow *Corvus corone*
..... Raven *Corvus corax*

## Sturnidae (Starlings)
..... Starling *Sturnus vulgaris*
..... Rose-coloured Starling *Sturnus roseus*

## Passeridae (Old World Sparrows)
..... House Sparrow *Passer domesticus*
..... Tree Sparrow *Passer montanus*
..... Rock Sparrow *Petronia petronia*

## Fringillidae (Siskins, Crossbills and Allies)
..... Chaffinch *Fringilla coelebs*
..... Brambling *Fringilla montifringilla*
..... Serin *Serinus serinus*
..... Greenfinch *Carduelis chloris*
..... Goldfinch *Carduelis carduelis*
..... Siskin *Carduelis spinus*
..... Linnet *Carduelis cannabina*
..... Twite *Carduelis flavirostris*
..... Common Redpoll *Carduelis flammea*
..... Lesser Redpoll *Carduelis cabaret*
..... Arctic Redpoll *Carduelis hornemanni*
..... Two-barred Crossbill *Loxia leucoptera*
..... Crossbill *Loxia curvirostra*
..... Parrot Crossbll *Loxia pytyopsittacus*
..... Common Rosefinch *Carpodacus erythrinus*
..... Bullfinch *Pyrrhula pyrrhula*
..... Hawfinch *Coccothraustes coccothraustes*

## Parulidae (New World Warblers)
..... Black-and-white Warbler *Mniotilta varia*

## Emberizidae (Buntings, Sparrows, Seedeaters and Allies)
..... Lark Sparrow *Chondestes grammacus*
..... White-throated Sparrow *Zonotrichia albicollis*
..... Lapland Bunting *Calcarius lapponicus*
..... Snow Bunting *Pletrophenax nivalis*
..... Pine Bunting *Emberiza leucocephalos*
..... Yellowhammer *Emberiza citrinella*
..... Cirl Bunting *Emberiza cirlus*
..... Ortolan Bunting *Emberiza hortulana*
..... Yellow-browed Bunting *Emberiza chrysophrys*
..... Rustic Bunting *Emberiza rustica*
..... Little Bunting *Emberiza pusilla*
..... Yellow-breasted Bunting *Emberiza aureola*
..... Reed Bunting *Emberiza schoeniclus*
..... Black-headed Bunting *Emberiza melanocephala*
..... Corn Bunting *Miliaria calandra*

## Additional species
..... ............................................................
..... ............................................................
..... ............................................................
..... ............................................................
..... ............................................................
..... ............................................................
..... ............................................................
..... ............................................................
..... ............................................................

## Useful addresses and contacts

### Birdline East Anglia
Call in news on 0800 083 0803 or 01603 163388
Email birdnews@birdline-eastanglia.co.uk
Web www.birdline-eastanglia.co.uk
Get News on 09068 700 245 (premiumm rate calls)
See Classifieds section for more details

### Broads Authority
18 Colegate
Norwich NR3 1BQ
Tel. 01603 610734
Fax 01603 765710
Web www.broads-authority.gov.uk/

### Cley Bird Club
Peter Gooden
45 Charles Road
Holt NR25 6DA
Tel. 01263 712368

### English Nature
60 Bracondale
Norwich NR1 2BE
Tel. 01603 620558
Fax 01603 762552
Web www.english-nature.org.uk/

### Great Yarmouth Bird Club
Keith R Dye
104 Wolseley Road
Great Yarmouth NR1 OEJ
Tel. 01493 600705
Web home.clara.net/ammodytes/gybirdclub.html

### Nar Valley Ornithological Society
Ian Black
Three Chimneys
Tumbler Hill
Swaffham PE37 7JG
Tel. 01760 724092
Email ian-a-black@hotmail.com

### Norfolk Bird Club
Vernon Eve
Pebble House
The Street
Syderstone
King's Lynn PE31 8SD
Tel. 01485 578121
Web www.norfolkbirdclub.org.uk/

### Norfolk Bird Recorder
Giles Dunmore
49 Nelson Road
Sheringham NR26 8DA
Tel. 01263 822550

### The Norfolk and Norwich Naturalists' Society
Dr Tony Leech
3 Eccles Road
Holt NR25 6HJ
Tel. 01263 712282
Web www.pastonroot.co.uk/golds/nnnshome.html

### The Norfolk Coast Project
6 Station Road
Wells-next-the-Sea NR23 1AE
Tel. 01328 711533
Fax 01328 710182
Email nor.coast@dial.pipex.com
Web www.norfolkcoastproject.org.uk/

### The Norfolk Ornithologists' Association
Jed Andrews
Broadwater Road
Holme next the Sea
Hunstanton PE36 6LQ
Tel. 01485 525406

### The Norfolk Wildlife Trust
72 Cathedral Close
Norwich NR1 4DF
Tel. 01603 625540
Fax 01603 630593
Email admin@nwt.cix.co.uk
Web www.wildlifetrust.org.uk/norfolk/

### The RSPB
East Anglia Regional Office
Stalham House
65 Thorpe Road
Norwich NR1 1UD
Tel. 01603 661662
Fax 01603 660088
Web www.rspb.org.uk

### Traveline East Anglia
(For all public transport enquiries)
Tel. 0870 608 2608
Web www.travelineeastanglia.org.uk/

# Index

## A

American Wigeon 72
Arctic Tern 37
Arctic Warbler 32, 75
Avocet 8, 18, 23, 26, 29, 36, 39, 43, 71

## B

Baird's Sandpiper 71
Banded Demoiselle 51, 87
Barn Owl 11, 23, 26, 28, 29, 36, 39, 49, 50, 53, 55, 57, 66, 72, 83
Barnhamcross Common 91
Barred Warbler 38
Barton Broad 48
Bean Goose 76
Bean (Taiga) Goose 64, 68
Bearded Tit 26, 27, 39, 53, 55, 57, 59, 66
Berney Marshes 71
Bewick's Swan 18, 19, 56
Birdline East Anglia 98
Birdwatcher's Code of Conduct 2
Bittern 39, 53, 55, 57, 62, 66, 67
Black Brant 30, 39
Black Redstart 70, 72, 75
Black-and-white Warbler 60
Black-headed Gull 41, 43, 67
Black-necked Grebe 32, 33, 71
Black-tailed Godwit 19
Black-winged Pratincole 26
Black-winged Stilt 26, 77
Blackborough rubbish tip 17
Blackcap 26
Blakeney Harbour 37
Blakeney Point 37
Blickling Lake 49
Blue-winged Teal 77
Bluethroat 38
Brambling 27
Brecks 79
Brent Goose 12, 29, 30, 36, 39
Breydon Water 73
Broads Authority 98
Brown Long-eared Bats 50
Buckenham Marsh 68
Bullfinch 26
Burnham Norton 29

## C

Cantley Marsh 68
Cantley Sugar Factory 70
Canvasback 19
Caspian Tern 71, 73
Cattle Egret 54
Cetti's Warbler 55, 57, 60, 63, 64, 66, 70
Chedgrave Marsh 76
Chiffchaff 26
Chinese Water Deer 64, 67
Choseley 28
Cley Bird Club 98
Cley Marshes NWT 38
Collared Pratincole 26, 72
Common Scoter 26
Common Buzzard 11, 44
Common Crane 53, 55
Common Hawker 58
Common Tern 26, 37, 50, 51
Common Sandpiper 60
Common Seals 27, 38
Cormorant 60
Corn Bunting 19, 28
Country Code 1
Crossbill 10, 79, 80, 82, 87, 88, 89
Cuckoo 23
Curlew 88
Curlew Sandpiper 8, 26

## D

Daubenton's Bat 60, 87
Dell 34
Dersingham Bog 10
Dusky Warbler 32, 75

## E

East Winch Common 17
East Wretham 87
Egyptian Goose 11, 16, 32, 33, 49, 50, 83
English Nature 98

## F

Filby Broad 62
Fishers Fleet 12
Flegg Broads 62
Flitcham and Abbey Farm 11

Franklin's Gull 26
Fulmar 6

**G**

Garden Warbler 26
Garganey 18, 19, 26, 36, 39, 41, 43, 68, 71
Glaucous Gull 12
Glossy Ibis 54
Goldcrest 31, 52, 88
Golden Oriole 67, 79, 80, 83
Golden Pheasant 10, 79, 80
Golden Plover 56, 72
Goldeneye 8, 32, 66
Goosander 47, 50, 66, 67
Goshawk 79, 80, 88, 89
Grasshopper Warbler 23, 25, 53, 55, 66, 68, 69
Grazing Marsh 30
Great Grey Shrike 86
Great Reed Warbler 72
Great Spotted Woodpecker 27
Great Yarmouth 74
Great Yarmouth Bird Club 98
Great Yarmouth cemetery 74
Greater Sandplover 74
Greater Yellowlegs 72, 74
Green Sandpiper 60
Green Woodpecker 13
Green-winged Teal 63
Greenish Warbler 32
Greenshank 8, 60
Grey Partridge 28
Grey Seal 38
Grey Wagtail 50, 51
Gunton Lake 47

**H**

Hairy Dragonfly 60, 67, 69, 72
Harbour Porpoise 58
Hawfinch 32, 79, 80, 82, 86, 91
Heacham 7
Hen Harrier 23, 26, 30, 36, 39, 53, 55, 58, 66, 67
Hickling Broad 53
Hobby 44, 59, 66, 67, 79, 80, 83
Holkham 30
Holkham Bay 30, 31
Holkham Grazing Marsh 30

Holkham Hall 32
Holkham Pines 31
Holme 23
Holme NOA Reserve 24
Holme NWT Reserve 25
Honey Buzzard 44
Horsey Mere 55
How Hill Nature Reserve 59
Hunstanton 6
Hume's Warbler 75

**I**

Isabelline Wheatear 58

**K**

Kellings Quags 43
Kentish Plover 73
Kestrel 44
Kingfisher 8, 11, 57, 60, 66, 70
Knot 8

**L**

Lady Anne's Drive 30
Lakenheath 83
Langley Marsh 76
Lapland Bunting 31, 41
Lapwing 29, 30, 36, 56, 72
Laughing Gull 26
Lesser Spotted Woodpecker 33, 49, 50, 66, 82, 86
Lesser White-fronted Goose 69
Lesser Whitethroat 26
Linnet 26
Little Owl 11, 28
Little Egret 26, 27, 53
Little Ringed Plover 60
Little Stint 8, 26
Little Tern 26, 37, 58, 74
Long-eared Owl 10
Long-tailed Duck 26
Lynford Arboretum 82
Lynn Point 12

**M**

Malthouse Broad 61
Marsh Harrier 12, 18, 26, 30, 36, 39, 53, 55, 57, 59, 63, 64, 66, 70
Marsh Sandpiper 47, 54, 69, 71

Marsh Tit 60, 66
Martham Broad 57
Massingham Heath 15
Mayday Farm 88
Mediterranean Gull 26, 36, 41, 74
Merlin 26, 39, 53, 55, 58, 72

**N**

Nar Valley Ornithological Society 98
Narborough 17
Natterjack Toad 25, 58
Night Heron 54
Nightingale 13, 17, 42
Nightjar 10, 13, 42, 58, 79, 80, 86,
    87, 88, 89
Noctule Bat 60
Norfolk and Norwich Naturalists'
    Society 98
Norfolk Bird Club 98
Norfolk Bird Recorder 98
Norfolk Coast Project 98
Norfolk Hawker 57, 60, 65, 67, 69, 72
Norfolk Ornithologists' Association 98
Norfolk Wildlife Trust 98
Nuthatch 32, 82, 86

**O**

Ormesby Broad 62
Osprey 50, 51, 59, 66
Otter 27
Ouse Washes 19
Oystercatcher 29, 36, 47, 51

**P**

Pallas's Warbler 25, 31, 32, 33, 52
passage migrants 7, 8, 29, 31, 33, 34,
    35, 37, 40, 43, 64, 71, 74
passage waders 36, 39, 41, 53, 55, 59,
    63, 66, 68, 70, 71, 73, 81
Penduline Tit 26
Pentney Gravel Pits 16
Peregrine 26, 68, 72
Pied Wheatear 58
Pied Flycatcher 35
Pied-billed Grebe 82
Pink-footed Goose 8, 11, 12, 30, 56, 72
Pipistrelle Bat 60
Pochard 19
Purple Sandpiper 6, 7, 74

**Q**

Quail 28

**R**

Radde's Warbler 32
Ranworth Broad 60
raptors 76
rarities 23, 34, 73
Red Kite 11
Red-breasted Merganser 8
Red-breasted Nuthatch 32
Red-eyed Damselfly 67
Red-flanked Bluetail 75
Red-necked Grebe 47
Red-rumped Swallow 58
Red-throated Diver 26
Redpoll 27, 60, 67, 82, 86
Redshank 29, 30, 36
Redstart 35, 87, 88
Reed Warbler 26, 29, 36
Richard's Pipit 41
Ring Ouzel 43, 59, 60
Ring-billed Gull 74
Rock Pipit 26
Rockland Broad 64
Roller 54
Rollesby Broad 62
Rose-coloured Starling 58
Ross's Gull 26
Rough-legged Buzzard 15, 58, 72, 76
Royal Society for the Protection of Birds
    (RSPB) 98
Roydon Common 13
Ruddy Duck 81
Ruff 60

**S**

Salthouse Beach Road 41
Salthouse Heath 42
Sandwich Tern 26, 37
Santon Downham 86
Savi's Warbler 53, 55, 63
Scarce Chaser 67, 69
Scarce Emerald Damselfly 82
sea duck 6
Sedge Warbler 26, 29, 36
Shelduck 47
Shorelark 23, 26, 31, 39, 41
Short-eared Owl 23, 26, 71, 72

Shoveler 72
Siberian Thrush 75
Siskin 27, 60, 67, 79, 80, 82, 86, 87, 88, 89
Skylark 88
Slavonian Grebe 26
Smew 17, 67
Snettisham 8
Snipe 30
Snow Bunting 26, 31, 39, 41
South Denes 74
Sparham Pools 50
Sparrowhawk 26, 44
Spoonbill 71
Spotted Flycatcher 51
Spotted Redshank 8
Stiffkey Fen 36
Stiffkey Woods 35
Stock Dove 32
Stone Curlew 79, 80, 85
Stonechat 58, 68
Strumpshaw Fen 66
Stubb Mill 54
Surf Scoter 26
Surlingham Church Marsh 63
Swallow 23
Swallowtail butterfly 55, 60, 62, 67
Swanton Novers 44

**T**
Tawny Owl 23, 32, 33, 87
Teal 72
Terek Sandpiper 72, 74
Thetford Warren 89
Thompson Water 81
thrushes 23, 37
Titchwell 26
Tottenhill Gravel Pits 17
Traveline East Anglia 98
Tree Pipit 13, 42, 79, 80, 87, 88, 89
Tree Sparrow 11, 19, 27, 28
Treecreeper 32, 86
Twite 26, 31, 39

**V**
Variable Damselfly 72
Velvet Scoter 26
visible migration 6, 23

**W**
waders 8, 12, 16, 18, 19, 26, 68, 70, 73, 83, 87
wagtails 37
Walsey Hills 40
warblers 18, 23, 26, 37, 40
Warham Greens 34
Water Pipit 68, 70
Water Rail 11, 26, 55
Water vole 27
Waxham 52
Wayland Wood 80
Weeting Heath 84
Wells Wood 30, 33
Welney 18
Wheatear 7, 23, 43, 85
Wheatfen Broad 65
Whimbrel 39
Whiskered Tern 65
White-fronted Goose 56, 64, 68
Whitethroat 26
Whooper Swan 18, 19, 56
Wigeon 30, 36, 68, 72
wildfowl 16, 18, 19, 29, 30, 47, 48, 49, 57, 60, 62, 64, 68, 70, 71, 73, 76, 77, 81
Willow Tit 59, 66, 67
Willow Warbler 26
Wilson's Phalarope 71
Winterton Dunes 58
Wolferton 10
Wood Sandpiper 60
Wood Warbler 59
Woodcock 13, 42, 59, 66, 79, 80, 86, 88, 89
woodland birds 47, 49, 50, 60, 80
Woodlark 13, 42, 79, 80, 85, 86, 88, 89
woodpeckers 32
Wroxham Broad 61
Wryneck 38

**Y**
Yellow Wagtail 41
Yellow-browed Warbler 25, 31, 33, 35, 52
Yellow-legged Gull 12
Yellowhammer 28